BETTER MEN
ON THE PATH TO PURITY

BETTER MEN

ON THE PATH TO PURITY

BISHOP PHILLIP H. PORTER JR.
WITH W. TERRY WHALIN

FOREWORD BY BILL McCARTNEY
FOUNDER OF PROMISE KEEPERS

ZondervanPublishingHouse
Grand Rapids, Michigan

A Division of HarperCollins*Publishers*

Better Men
Copyright © 1998 by Phillip H. Porter Jr. and W. Terry Whalin

Requests for information should be addressed to:

 ZondervanPublishingHouse
Grand Rapids, Michigan 49530

Library of Congress Cataloging-in-Publication Data

Porter, Phillip.
    Better men : on the path to purity / Phillip H. Porter, Jr. with W. Terry
Whalin
      p.   cm.
    Includes bibliographical references.
    ISBN 0-310-21785-7 (softcover)
    Men—Religious life. 2. Promise Keepers (Organization). I. Whalin,
Terry. II. Title.
    BV4528.2.P67 1997
    248.8'42—dc21   97-41432
                                                    CIP

Interior design by Sherri L. Hoffman

Printed in the United States of America

---

98 99 00 01 02 03 04 /❖ DC/ 10 9 8 7 6 5 4 3 2 1

CONTENTS

FOREWORD

IN THE EARLY DAYS OF PROMISE KEEPERS, I heard that Phillip Porter was a leader in the African American community and that I should meet with him. Other people told me that Bishop Porter was a good and fair man, so we scheduled a meeting at his All Nations Church.

My version about our first meeting is different from Phil's. The minute that I saw him, I liked him. While Phil acted as if he was angry with me, I could tell that this man loved Jesus too much to stay mad at someone else who loved Jesus. I was never intimidated by his initial arms-length approach. Instead, I could see despite his gruff exterior that I was going to have a good relationship with this wonderful man.

When I learned that I had offended him and others in the African American community (I will let him explain what happened), it was very easy for me to submit to Phil. I dropped to my knees and asked his forgiveness. He is a humble man of God.

Please pay attention to what Phil has to say because he has a wealth of experience. Regardless of life's contradictions, Phil has come through with love in his heart. Life has served up a lot of curveballs to Bishop Porter. In the pages of this book you will see that he has met many people who have not lived out their promises. Yet he has come through life's disappointments with his heart still centered on Jesus

Christ. Unlike many others, Phil's focus has not been stuck on these disappointments; instead he continues to look at his Savior. Because Phil looks at Jesus, he looks at others through eyes of love.

With an articulate manner of expressing his thoughts, Phil is bright and perceptive. He is one of the men to whom God has given the gift of saying the right thing at the right time. I have spent hours one-on-one with Phil because of his role as the chairman of the Promise Keepers board of directors. From my experience, I know Phil is going to be genuinely interested in you and your position. He will always approach you with caution, honor, and respect. Phil won't be aggressive with his own opinions or impose his doctrines on you. But if you ask, you will discover that he has incredible wisdom. Phil is a wonderful blend of a man who is kind and gentle with a soft spirit.

As much as I love Phil Porter, let's not give him too much credit. Let's give God the credit for what He has done through Phil's life. Read, pray, and think through the words in this book, because Bishop Porter has lived through some challenging life experiences and has earned the right to speak to you about key spiritual issues along your path to purity.

—BILL MCCARTNEY
Founder of Promise Keepers
Boulder, Colorado

CHAPTER ONE

A SEARCH FOR TRUE SPIRITUALITY

THE DUST BILLOWED BEHIND THE 1950 CHEVROLET as we roared down the highway. My necktie felt a little snug around my neck, but overall I was pretty comfortable in my suit. Several times a week I tied that knot around my neck. Today I was headed for a different kind of bind. On my lap were the notes for my speech, and on either side of me sat two white women from the Women's Christian Temperance Union (WCTU) in Enid, Oklahoma. It wasn't even eight o'clock in the morning, but already it felt as if something different was about to happen.

A few weeks earlier, Mrs. Thompson had invited me to speak for the WCTU on Reconciliation Sunday. Back in 1953, the WCTU fought gallantly against the evils of alcohol and tobacco. The organization ran essay contests, and because I always entered those contests, I received a lot of invitations to speak at WCTU gatherings. Throughout north central Oklahoma, I spoke to civic groups such as Kiwanis, Rotary, and Lions Clubs. But on this day I could sense a change in the air even as the dust blew behind our car.

The little country church where we stopped looked like something on a magazine cover—picture perfect with a small picket fence around part of the yard, and a bell on a steeple. The church stood on a corner lot just off Highway 64 in a small town west of Enid. This and the other towns around there had a reputation for fierce racial prejudice and being diligent about enforcing the segregation policies.

As a sixteen-year-old, I felt nervous about speaking to all these white people. Yet I managed to calm my fears, thinking, *These ladies from the WCTU know what they are doing. Besides, I'm speaking at their invitation.*

When I entered the building, I could see that while I was the choice of the WCTU, I was *not* the choice of the congregation. Some people turned red in embarrassment at my arrival. I saw other people bristle at my entrance. These people were in church, but I could see that their attention was elsewhere than on the things of God. During the opening prayers and songs, I sat on the platform and looked over the audience. Then the leader of the WCTU introduced me as the speaker, and I moved to the podium.

As I began to speak, two men stood up and walked to the back. With a great stir, the men—who, I learned later, were deacons and leaders in the congregation—signaled their protest that a colored person would speak at their church. One of the men silently motioned to the WCTU leader. She walked to the back of the auditorium and talked with the men.

"Yes," she whispered, "what can I do for you?"

"That nigger," one whispered in her ear and gestured in my direction. "Why did you bring him? You need to cut him short. We don't want to listen to him speak on reconciliation. We find it offensive."

"We selected Phillip Porter for today's speaker," the woman calmly replied. "I will not stop him from speaking."

"We'll see about that," the man groused. The WCTU leader turned and went back to her seat. I had spoken amid some commotion on other occasions, and I knew this stir probably had something to do with me. The audience was more uncomfortable than I was. For my WCTU speeches, I was accustomed to being the only black present.

During my message I recalled an incident from my childhood. My earliest memories as I was growing up in Oklahoma were of being in church. Sunday morning was segregated throughout the state and the rest of the nation. That hour of worship has often been called "the most segregated hour of the week" in the United States; it was then, and it remains so today. Blacks went to their church with their own style of worship while white people attended their services. In those days, segregation wasn't unusual; it was the norm.

"The Gospels in the New Testament tell us about the church during Jesus' day," I said. "The people in those days were separated during the day, but one of the Jewish leaders approached Jesus Christ at night. Nicodemus was a respected leader who didn't want to be seen with this miracle man during the daylight. Nevertheless, Nicodemus recognized Jesus as the Messiah and asked Jesus what he had to do in order to be born again. This significant conversation happened under the cloak of darkness.

"On Sunday evenings in Enid, I've seen a reconciliation among the races that doesn't happen on Sunday morning. During the cloak of darkness, there is something occurring," I said. I then described how, at our small congregation of the Church of God in Christ, my family gathered with people across racial lines for a worship service. The faces in the audience were a mixture. White people sat beside black people, Native Americans beside white people.

"In those services, we had no 'Negro' pews. Instead, our focus was on who we came to worship. Through our music, we lifted the One who transcended race or creed—the Lord Jesus Christ. And in those days, when the preacher delivered the message, color didn't make any difference. From all over the congregation, people said an 'Amen' or 'That's right, Brother.'"

I looked over my white audience on this Sunday afternoon and continued. "At the end of these services, when the pastor gave the invitation, whites, blacks, Native Americans, and even a few Hispanics poured down the aisle to the front of the church, then knelt at the altar. Everyone needed a touch from God in their lives—for healing, for salvation, and for strength to make it through the week ahead. The supply from God was available and readily accessible.

"Why at night?" I challenged the audience. "Does such a mixture only have to occur under the cloak of darkness? We're here for Reconciliation Sunday, and it looks like we have a long ways to go for reconciliation to take place in our churches. . . ."

As a young black student, I knew that the barriers between people could be removed. From these childhood experiences, I knew that Jesus Christ could empower people to forget about skin color. I painted a picture of equality in God's kingdom and equal opportunity for all people—no matter which race or background. In the eyes of God, our playing field was perfectly level.

As I worked the audience with my best oratory skills, I could see the agitation and disbelief on their faces. Those two white deacons were still pacing in the back of the room, trying to create a way to stop me from speaking.

Out of the corner of my eye, I saw the two men motion to their pastor. Reluctantly the elderly man rose from his seat and walked to the back of the room. "Get that nigger off the platform or you'll be looking for a new church!" one man proclaimed in a loud whisper.

Given the influence of this deacon, the pastor knew it was not an idle threat. He motioned for the WCTU leader and explained the situation. A few minutes later, Mrs. Thompson handed me a note. While I continued to speak, I opened it and read, "Finish your talk in three minutes." I quickly completed my message.

After the conclusion of the service, I walked to the back of the church and greeted the congregation. Some were polite but cool. Others walked past with angry looks. These white folks were probably thinking, *Why, the very idea of this colored boy speaking at our nice, little, white church on Sunday! And what boldness for him to talk about reconciliation.*

As the crowd broke up, the two women from the WCTU took me home. While driving down the highway, they had tears streaming down their faces and their voices trembled. I learned why my speech had been suddenly cut short. "It wasn't you, Phillip," one of the women explained. "You did a good job, but we're living in difficult times. People aren't ready to listen to what you have to say."

From God's perspective, these women were ahead of their time. To them, the color of a person's skin wasn't important. They were ready to receive spiritual truth from whoever would give them truth. They were more concerned about the contents than about the messenger. Did the words ring true to God and the Bible? These two women chose to ask this question instead of focusing on outward appearance.

On another occasion, these two ladies took me to another town. My speech was interrupted and became more of a discussion than an address. One man spoke up: "We don't have any Negroes in this town. So how do you think we can be friends with them? The only people of race that we have in this area are a few Mexican-Americans and some Indians. And all the Indians want to do is to scalp us."

My dialogue with this man didn't lead to anything worthwhile. As I left this small Oklahoma town, I knew their walls of separation were firmly in place. And today that wall is still pretty much intact.

For more than forty years I have been speaking on reconciliation and working with people—black and white—who want to heal the nation's racial divisions. We have made some progress in this matter, but sadly, there are still churches that refuse to welcome people of color. The reality and truth of 2 Corinthians 5:17–18 needs to break through and change our lives: "Therefore, if anyone is in Christ, he is a new creation; the old has gone, the new has come! All this is from God, who reconciled us to himself through Christ and gave us the *ministry of reconciliation*." It was *in Christ* that God was reconciling the world to himself. And because we are *in Christ*, God has committed to us that ministry of a spiritual connection to each other.

As a teenager I spoke often about equality—yet nothing in my world seemed to change. Separation and strong feelings of prejudice were firmly in place in these small Oklahoma towns. Could it ever be changed?

One day in my teens, I was discussing this unchanging wall of prejudice with my mother. I said, "I'm going to quit making these speeches, Momma. We talk and talk, but nothing seems to get done." But Momma wouldn't hear of it. Whenever I received an invitation to speak to a group of white people, Momma always encouraged me to go. She told me, "What rich opportunities you have, Phillip! I didn't have these opportunities, and your daddy didn't have these invitations. Many other black people haven't been invited, but you have been selected. Go and take advantage of it and do all of the speaking that you can."

Momma gave me a vision for helping people get beyond the barriers of race and prejudice, and her vision continues to drive my life and work.

A SPIRITUAL HUNGER AMONG MEN

THESE DAYS, I AM STILL SPEAKING about reconciliation, but I have been given a new platform. It is called Promise Keepers, and at first I wasn't very impressed.

One August afternoon in 1991, I sat in my office chair at my church—the All Nations Pentecostal Center Church of God in Christ. In irritation, I was rocking my chair back and forth, anticipating my next meeting. In a few minutes some men from this group called Promise Keepers would arrive at the church.

Several days earlier, someone from the organization had called and made an appointment.

"We're looking for some African American leaders to join our organization," they had said.

"Fine! Come on down," I answered.

While I didn't know much about the group, I knew that their founder was Coach Bill McCartney from the University of Colorado (CU). In the last few weeks I had been searching for a means to make a strong move *against* Coach McCartney.

Only a few days earlier, an African American tailback with the CU Buffaloes, Eric Bieniemy, had been arrested. Bieniemy had allegedly assaulted a firefighter from Aurora, Colorado, at the home of Eric's mother. As a leader in the black community, I had been asked to help Bieniemy. Although the football season had not yet started, the local and national sportswriters had been touting Bieniemy as a contender for the prestigious Heisman Trophy. That would have been quite an honor for this boy who had grown up in a poor section of Los Angeles, California, known as Watts.

Now, with Eric having been suspended for the first couple of games, other African Americans and I feared that the tailback would lose his opportunity for the Heisman. I thought, *Why the nerve of this white coach to jeopardize the chance of a lifetime for this highly motivated kid!* To me, it looked as if Coach Mac had suspended Eric as a reaction to pressure from the media and the CU alumni.

The more I learned about Bieniemy's arrest, the more I felt that the accusations against him had racial undertones. The event as I learned it was that when a fire broke out at his mother's house, Eric and some other CU players extinguished the blaze. Amid the commotion, someone in the neighborhood called the fire department and the police. When the firemen arrived, immediately one of them jumped off the fire engine, grabbed an ax, and began to tear into the fire-scarred garage wall.

"Stop! We've put out the fire!" Eric yelled. Then he took a natural step for a football player: He dislodged the fireman from his ax. While the two men were struggling, the police arrived and arrested Bieniemy. Two weeks later, Coach McCartney announced that Bieniemy would be suspended from the football team's first game.

On August 20, I appeared in Aurora Municipal Court with Bieniemy. The football player pleaded no contest and was sentenced to forty hours of community service, which he performed at All Nations Church. From my perspective, Eric's suspension was not necessary. I tried to think of a way to get this white coach's attention. Now this meeting with Promise Keepers looked like my perfect chance.

Right on schedule, several men from Promise Keepers arrived at the church and sat in the basement. To my surprise, Coach McCartney was among the group. For several minutes I listened patiently as the men explained the overall goals of Promise Keepers and their desire to reach the African American community. They briefly reviewed the seven promises of a Promise Keeper. In particular, they emphasized the sixth promise—to reach beyond any racial and denominational barriers to demonstrate the power of biblical unity.

As they talked, I felt my inner tension increase. Finally I had had enough and couldn't stand it anymore—especially this talk about reconciliation.

"Why, the audacity of you to come and talk with us about reconciliation and prejudice when you have acted against one of our African American football players!" I said to the men. "It's just another case of white men against black."

Initially everyone was bewildered at my sudden response. Finally Coach Mac said, "Are you talking about Eric Bieniemy?"

"Yes," I said with force. "You immediately suspended him without rhyme or reason. It's another case of taking these players and just using them."

"Oh, no!" Coach Mac protested. "You don't understand. I followed a rule that we have which suspends anyone when they are arrested or jailed. Each player knows these rules, and it doesn't discriminate against blacks."

Then Coach thought for a few seconds about the university's rules. He realized that more black players than white were being arrested in Boulder, Colorado, and therefore suffered to a greater degree the penalty inflicted by the rules.

"Oh, God, I could be wrong!" Coach said. Sliding out of his chair, Coach McCartney knelt before me. "I never meant to do anything wrong against my black brothers, and I apologize. More than apologizing here in this private meeting, I promise to apologize publicly."

As this strong white man knelt in front of me, I started to gloat inside with a feeling of pride that I had acted so strongly for my African American community. Suddenly the Holy Spirit spoke to my own heart about this situation: "You're just as guilty. While Coach offended you from lack of knowledge, you are acting out of prejudice toward him."

As I attempted to argue with the Holy Spirit based on my race and background, I found I was no match for the Spirit of truth. That Spirit convinced me I had prejudged out of my ignorance and preconception of the facts.

Coach insisted on staying on his knees until I pulled him up.

"All right," I said, "at least I'm beginning to understand your reason for suspending Eric."

While Coach had apparently committed an act of prejudice against the black community, I was equally guilty. The Spirit of God showed me that without a second thought, I was prejudiced against Coach's actions. I had fallen into the old thought pattern that says, "Everybody who is not your color is your enemy." I automatically believed that this white man was acting prejudicially against all blacks. So I also needed to repent, and I did, and Coach Mac forgave me.

Now Coach and I were reconciled, and our feelings of prejudice disappeared.

The meeting shifted to a discussion of how Promise Keepers could gain cooperation from the African American community in Denver.

"You don't understand the first thing about how our Ministerial Alliance of African American pastors works," I explained. "I can't decide to be the African American representative for Promise Keepers on my own initiative. The Alliance must choose the person to serve on your board. Otherwise it's not right."

"Well, Dr. Porter," the men said. "We want you to serve on the Promise Keepers board. How can we present this information to the Alliance?"

Several weeks later, the African American Ministerial Alliance met for breakfast. Coach McCartney attended and listened as the ministers talked about their dreams and plans for the inner city. Coach Mac, in a clear and transparent fashion, told the group how he wanted the Promise Keeper organization to represent men of color—at the highest level of the organization, including its leadership. The African American pastors could see that Coach wasn't putting on a show but that this desire was sincere.

Eventually the Alliance selected two men—Dick Clark, a Christian businessman and social activist, and me—to serve on the fifteen-member board of directors of Promise Keepers. Clark is the former director of the Denver World Poverty Program. He is a layman who is well connected to the concerns of the African American community from a Christian perspective.

During my first year with Promise Keepers I was elected vice chairman, and since June 1994 I have been chairman of the board.

Promise Keepers has become an international movement. In early 1996, I traveled to both South Africa and India for the organization. The group of us who went to South Africa attended a luncheon that had been set up in an exclusive Afrikaans club in Johannesburg. This club was located in an exclusive white neighborhood. Our hosts comprised the three ethnic groups in the nation: Afrikaans of Dutch descent, Africans—the natives of the land—and Colored, the crossbreeds. While we were waiting outside this club, one of the Coloreds in the group, a man named James, asked me a question that no one in the United States had posed to me.

"Tell me, Bishop Porter. As proud as we are of you being the chairman of the board, aren't you really a token?" James said.

At first, the boldness of the question surprised me, but it was a sincere query that deserved a thoughtful response. I smiled and said, "James, thanks for asking that question. I should admit that even in my country, no one has asked me that question. No one had the gall to ask it. I had to come all the way to South Africa for you to ask me about this important topic."

I continued, "By my own nature, I could never be a token African American. Though some may have that opinion, we're working hard to dispel that. For me, a token is someone who simply fills a spot because of a need to be politically correct. I've never filled spots in my life. Instead, I enter a position and attempt to make things happen. A token doesn't have any power for change. I'm not just window dressing."

As we stood outside that South African club, I told James how I came into Promise Keepers in the first place. I wouldn't let the group select me to fill a spot as a token. Instead, my position on the board of this organization had to come from the community. Because I was selected from my community, I also have a responsibility to report to them on a regular basis. I am in continual contact with the African American leaders in my community so that they can identify and give me feedback about my actions. In the true sense of the word, I am a representative of my race—not a token.

In 1990, only 72 men met together, but Promise Keepers quickly blossomed into the fastest-growing men's movement in the nation. During 1995, the thirteen massive national rallies had a combined attendance of 720,000 men. During 1996, Promise Keepers reached 1.2 million men in twenty-three rallies. These rallies are held in some of America's best-known stadiums: New York's Shea Stadium, Chicago's Soldier Field, the Los Angeles Coliseum, the Seattle Kingdome, the Minneapolis Metrodome, Washington's RFK Stadium, and Denver's Mile High Stadium. With capacities ranging from 40,000 to 60,000, many of these summer events are sold out well ahead of time. This growth has been covered in major media, including news magazines such as *Time*, *Newsweek*, and *U.S. News and World Report*, television networks such as ABC News, and numerous pages on the World Wide Web.

Why is this movement happening? Essentially, Promise Keepers is a Christ-centered ministry dedicated to uniting men to become a godly influence in their world. The values of the organization are captured in seven promises. These promises are not a new list of commandments, but a clarion call for men to return to their Creator. The opening pages of

Genesis tell us that man was created in the image of God. Mankind in its different parts reflects the Creator God.

The Hebrew language uses four main words for *man*. The first word is *adam*, which means "human." The second is translated *ish*, which means maleness and is logically paired with the feminine form *ishah*, which refers to woman. Genesis 2:23 says, "She shall be called *ishah*, for she was taken out of *ish*." For men, the word, *ish* conveys a sense of dignity and strength and, in fact, it is from this word that the concept of "gentleman" developed. Our *ish* factor is given from God and is a part of our creation from God. If a man turns from following the Creator and divides his attention, he becomes embroiled in conflict. Because we have strayed into different conflicts and away from God, we are not as pure as we are called to be.

Promise Keepers has recognized that for a man to return to his original connection with the Creator God, he must identify and return to the Source of Life. This men's movement—a movement of God's Spirit—has set a standard for what it means to be a godly man in today's world. A godly man lives his life with a fresh standard that includes honesty, integrity, and commitment—all biblical values that men need to recover and restore.

SEVEN PATHS TO PURITY

IN THIS BOOK I DISCUSS SEVEN PATHS to purity. In our world, the path to purity is obscured by barriers and obstacles. Each of these seven paths will carry us to a deeper spiritual relationship and a more reliable direction for living.

The first path to purity is to find a spiritual connection. Unless first things are put first, the path to purity will be obscured by bushes and brambles.

"No man is an island"—as John Donne wrote—but each of us needs friends. The second path to purity addresses this need for men to be in relationship with other men. I will tell about my own experience in finding a vital relationship with other men.

The third path to purity addresses several gray areas of life. In a world where deception and lies are promoted as the pathway to success, I will show how I have been able to practice sexual, moral, ethical, and spiritual purity.

For men to follow the fourth path to purity will mean a commitment to marriage and family through love, protection, and biblical values. Reverence for the sanctity of marriage will preserve our homes. In a world with a skyrocketing divorce rate, I want to offer some solid tools for protecting our greatest investment.

The fifth path to purity means finding a place to grow strong spiritually. If we remove a log from a fire, that fire will slowly use up all its fuel until it dies. In the spiritual realm, we need to grow spiritually in the local church. Through recounting personal experiences I want to lead us toward some everyday solutions for keeping us on the right track.

The sixth path to purity addresses one of the rising tensions in our everyday world—barriers. I will describe my own journey in seeking to lower racial and denominational barriers through spiritual solutions.

The final path to purity involves influence and confronts a critical question that tends to get lost in the masses and the busyness of everyday living: Can one man make a difference in our world? If we follow the last path to purity, we can learn to love our neighbors as ourselves and have a deepening effect on the world around us. These principles have been evident in my own life.

In summary, these are some of the questions the next chapters will address:

- How can a man find a spiritual connection?
- How can a man find other committed men for an accountable relationship?
- How can a man live with integrity—morally, ethically, sexually, and spiritually?
- How can a man become the spiritual leader of his home and honor his wife and children?
- How can a man find a place to grow spiritually?
- How can a man break through the barriers of race, prejudice, and denominationalism?
- How can one man make a difference in his world?

These are critical days for men in the United States. I believe there are many hopeful signs on the horizon. The winds of change are blowing. For you, change may begin with a single step of commitment.

CHAPTER TWO

THE ROOT OF THE PROBLEM

MISSING. EMPTY. LONELY. The words captured the root of J.J.'s problem. While J.J. never slowed down enough to pinpoint a reason, something was obviously absent from his life. Maybe what he needed were the basic icons of youthful satisfaction—more money and a good-looking set of wheels. When the drug dealers offered their wares to J.J., he resisted at first. Then he began using drugs on a casual basis. Casual turned into a habit. Soon he started selling drugs to others. A natural salesman, J.J. soon found that money was the least of his worries. As long as he was pushing product, he had plenty of money and managed to buy that set of wheels—with cash. Yet money didn't fill the void in his life.

On the other side of the country, Pete had some of the same feelings as J.J. Inside he felt empty, but instead of money, Pete tried the corporate world. He graduated with honors from college at the perfect time, when large corporations were looking to hire African Americans for crucial positions. Pete was well qualified. He jumped into the world of international banking and began to climb the ladder of success. The cost in terms of time and energy and ethics was of no concern to Pete. He was headed to the top no matter what it took, so he worked long hours and devoted himself to the workplace. Yet that empty feeling didn't disappear.

In the inner city of Detroit, another man had embarked on a different search. In his 'hood, Andrew knew who had the power. It wasn't the police; rather, it was gang members. In junior high school, Andrew began hanging out with a gang. Andrew was smart and could handle his fists pretty well, so before long he was one of the leaders. Feeling an adrenaline rush, Andrew reveled in the power he could hold over people. He led the gang to burglarize small businesses and even started killing people. While he felt a rush from using power, the rush was only temporary. It didn't take long before Andrew was on the prowl for another charge of power. Why this search, and what was he looking for to fill this need?

Many men are on a spiritual search. This quest is reflected in the bumper sticker that reads, HE WHO DIES WITH THE MOST TOYS WINS. To get these toys, we work long hours—but do they fill our needs? The only distinction between men and boys is the size of their toys. Instead of the latest action figure, men try to acquire a larger home, a bigger or nicer car, and that country club membership.

Yet J.J., Pete, Andrew, and the hundreds of men like them won't find the way to fill the void through money, work, or power.

Nor are they the only ones with the problem. That same kind of emptiness can be found in abundance within the walls of our churches. Some men join the stadium throngs at Promise Keepers events because of the good feeling they take home—and then immediately discard. Others come for the Bible teaching and the uplifting times of worship— good reasons in themselves, but hardly sufficient as a primary motivation. Other men carry this search into their service within the church. They join every committee and come to the church every time the door is open. Through their consistent service, they believe they are filling some void in life. But service to the church by itself will not provide the answer.

Don't get me wrong. Encouraging revivals, attending church, serving on committees, and helping the church however possible are good—if accomplished with the right motivation and reason. The great philosopher Pascal observed that inside every man is a hole that only God can fill. At the very core, man is essentially a spiritual being. Our search to fill the God-created vacuum leads us in many directions. But from my experience as well as that of millions of others, there is only one right road—a personal relationship with Jesus Christ.

FIRST THINGS FIRST

AS WE GIVE JESUS CHRIST the first place in our lives, we fill our spiritual void. I was reminded of this truth recently when I found an old cassette tape that my dad and mom recorded in 1959—the year I graduated from college. My fingers trembled as I held the tape that carried the words of my father. Some of my children and grandchildren and my wife, Lee, gathered around our living room. With a sense of anticipation I put the cassette into the tape recorder and pushed the play button. My father and mother passed away many years ago, but their voices filling that room took me back to a foundational principle for my life: First things first. On the tape my dad read Matthew 6:33: "Seek ye first the kingdom of God, and his righteousness; and all these things shall be added unto you" (KJV). It was modeled and taught in my family to have your priorities straight.

Throughout my life, when I have faced difficult and sometimes unexpected circumstances, I have turned to God. For example, when I graduated from college with a degree in social work, I accepted a job in a small Colorado town. The office had confirmed my job with a letter. Leaving my wife and two children temporarily in Oklahoma, I traveled on a bus to Walsenburg. Although my appointment wasn't until Monday, I arrived on the previous Thursday to visit the office and meet my co-workers. I entered the workplace and introduced myself: "Hello, I'm Phillip Porter, and I'm here for the job."

My presence caused a stir among the workers, but I didn't make much of it. The supervisor came to the front of the office and told me, "I'm sorry, but that job has been filled." His words didn't put me off, because I knew that I was the one who had filled the job.

"Yes," I said. "I'm the one who has filled the job. In fact, I've got a letter here to prove it." I reached into my suit coat and pulled out the letter from the supervisor. It gave details such as my job description, a time to report for my interview, and the supervisor's name.

"No, the job has been filled," the supervisor said as he reached across and snatched the letter from my hands. As I watched in horror, he tore the letter into small pieces and dropped it into the trash can. "There is no position here." Evidently, the office had expected me to be a white student from an all-white school. I had lost the job because I was black.

In shock, I turned and walked out of the office. *What would I do now? I had no plan B. A great number of people in my hometown of Enid had sent me off with excitement. What in the world would I tell them? My wife and kids were counting on this job, and now the door had slammed shut.* My only recourse was to turn to God. Because of my relationship with God, I had a place to turn when I hit such an unexpected event in my life.

Everyone has bumps along life's path. When something unexpected happens, where do you turn for help? When we don't first seek God, we put our trust in the wrong things and expect everything else to fall into place and then wonder why it doesn't work. We depend on our education, our intellect, or our ability to earn money. Or we put our personal desires and ambitions ahead of God's direction for our lives. These "things" take God's place and become our focus for life. Then when situations swirl out of control, we wonder, "What went wrong?" Sound familiar?

My father's voice on the tape continued with a brief explanation of Matthew 6:33: "What things, my son? What are the things you have need of? What are the things you desire?" Without really choosing it, this verse has become the foundation stone of my life. Until I found this tape, I could not give a reason why Matthew 6:33 is my favorite passage in the Bible. The congregation of my church will readily tell you, however, that this passage constantly appears in my sermons because it means so much to me. My dad was reminding us, "Put first things first. God is concerned about the necessities of your life."

When we set a high priority on our relationship with Jesus Christ and give Him first place in everyday living, He fills any void or emptiness. We can feel whole because of our connection to Christ and His heavenly Father. As we give our daily affairs to God, He directs our steps. Psalm 37:23 says,

> If the LORD delights in a man's way,
>   he makes his steps firm.

Notice how this promise from God comes with a condition: The Lord must "delight in our way." We have to make the first move and commit our daily actions into God's hands. This is the initial step along the path to purity—a commitment to honor Jesus Christ.

The psalmist continues with some promises that result as we delight in God:

> Though he stumble, he will not fall,
>   for the LORD upholds him with his hand.
> I was young and now I am old,
>   yet I have never seen the righteous forsaken
>   or their children begging bread.
> They are always generous and lend freely;
>   their children will be blessed. (vv. 24–26)

As we commit our lives to God—every day—we will have sufficient resources in our lives to help others. We can endure and conquer any kind of trouble or distress. As we honor Jesus Christ, we have a new standard for measurement—not materialism, but the Bible.

Now I can almost see your eyes slam shut and hear your ears close. I guess I *am* sounding like a preacher. And I realize that pointing you to the Bible sounds like an easy way out. I guess it makes sense to me because I have read it all my life. But I also know that it works. It is God's instruction manual for us, but it won't do any good sitting unopened on the dresser.

Here are four steps to take that will strengthen your relationship with Jesus Christ and restore your spiritual life.

Read the Bible Consistently. While the Bible is the world's best-selling book, it probably is not the most used. Make sure you select a modern translation for your reading that will speak to your needs in your language—the New International Version, the New King James Version, or the Living Bible. Try reading several different versions until you find one that you can readily identify with, understand, and enjoy.

Begin your reading with the stories in the Bible. Start with the gospel of Mark and the simple stories in the Old and New Testaments. The instruction manual for any book has to be introduced in its basic components. If you give attention to the basics, it will give you foundational truth. The stories of the Bible may have happened many years ago, but they are as fresh as today's newspaper. For example, God described King David as a "man after his own heart." Now, David wasn't a saint and, in fact, the Bible tells us that he had an affair with Bathsheba (see 2 Samuel 11). She got pregnant. David knew he had disobeyed God's laws, so he reacted the way many of us would: He tried to cover it up. The king sent for Bathsheba's husband, Uriah, who was a soldier out on the battlefield. He thought that Uriah would respond like most men who have not seen their wives for a long time. David thought, *Uriah will go straight to bed with his wife and have sex!*

Unfortunately, Uriah didn't follow the king's plan. Instead, he slept in the street outside the king's palace. When David asked Uriah about it, the soldier responded that he couldn't conscientiously have sex with his wife while a battle was raging. So the king sent Uriah back to the battle. He carried a special message for the commander: "Put this man in the front line so he will be killed." As the king intended, Uriah died in the heat of battle.

After Uriah's death, David married Bathsheba. But the baby that was conceived in their affair died shortly after its birth. How's that for real-life drama? But don't just stop with the story. Think about what it means to you personally. Even with his faults, David was called a man after God's own heart because he was constantly humbled by his sins, then repented, and sought the face of God for another opportunity. Reading the Bible will help you understand how God works in our lives. He will forgive and love you just as He did with David.

In Psalm 119:9–11 David asks a pressing question that we continue to ask today: "How can a young man keep his way pure?" Immediately an answer is provided. "By living according to [God's] word." While the answer is simple and straightforward, how do we do that in detail? "I seek you with all my heart; do not let me stray from your commands." Notice how David follows his desire to seek God with a quick cry for help: Don't let me stray from your commands or stray from the path of God. Finally, David gives us the key to seeing these changes happen on the inside: "I have hidden your word in my heart that I might not sin against you." The words from the Bible keep us from sin. Our first step is to read them consistently; then, when we face temptation or any other situation in our daily lives, we have a new resource—the words of God.

Study the Bible. Beyond reading the Bible, a second way to consistently learn about God is to study the Bible. We always need the right tool for a job. We would never consider trying to trim the bushes in our yard with a butcher knife—there are better tools for cutting bushes. In the same way, there are excellent tools for studying the Scriptures and helping us to understand them. When you start reading some sections of Paul's letters or other books in the Bible, a good commentary or concordance or study Bible will be useful. Select a book of the Bible in which you have some interest, then study it with some reference books, a journal for taking notes, and a pen. By taking notes on a particular section or writing down your thoughts, you have some additional tools for reflecting on what you have learned.

Take a small section of a book in the Bible—for example, the first verses of Philippians. As you look at these verses, ask yourself:

—What do the verses say?
—Is there some cultural information about the Philippian church in a reference book that will help me understand?
—What are these verses saying to me, or how can I apply these verses in my everyday situation?

As you study the Bible on a consistent basis, you will increase your knowledge about God and also strengthen your personal relationship with Christ.

Let me caution you to make sure you set a reasonable goal for yourself to keep from getting discouraged. Some men try to study an hour a night when they don't have that sort of time. Or they push themselves to complete a book in a particular time frame. Relax! There is no pressure to do things within a certain amount of time; instead, simply study for the joy of knowing more about God.

The study of God's Word will enrich your life. Consider the words of the prophet Jeremiah: "When your words came, I ate them; they were my joy and my heart's delight, for I bear your name, O Lord God Almighty" (Jeremiah 15:16). To consume and study God's Word answers a longing of our hearts. As the old song says, "I cried and I cried all night long, yet my soul just couldn't be content until I found the Lord. So I moaned and I moaned and I moaned all night long, yet my soul just couldn't be content until I found the Lord." As we study God's Word, He will stir up a hunger so we can learn more about Him.

Memorize the Bible. A third way to learn more about God is to memorize the Bible. I often encounter resistance to this suggestion: "Not me! I haven't memorized Bible verses since I was small." Or, "I can hardly remember some phone numbers, much less verses from the Bible."

I suggest that, as with the first two strategies for learning about God, you begin in a small way. Some verses are easy to memorize, such as John 14:6: "Jesus answered, 'I am the way and the truth and the life. No one comes to the Father except through me.'" Write the verse down on a small piece of paper or note card and tuck it into your shirt pocket. Then whenever you have a few spare minutes, such as at a stoplight, look at the verse. It won't be long until you can say the entire verse. Learn a verse perfectly before you start another verse. Again, it is helpful to use a contemporary translation. After you have memorized a verse, review it to keep it in the forefront of your mind. If you want some detailed teaching about memorizing verses, I suggest *The Topical Memory System* (NavPress) as an excellent method.

There are numerous benefits to memorizing God's Word. First, it will give you confidence in talking with others about the Bible and spiritual matters. Second, memorizing verses takes our minds off ourselves and focuses them on God and His direction for our lives. Finally, memorizing verses keeps us from sin. When you face temptation, you can turn to the words of Jesus, who, when tempted by Satan, said, "Man does not live on bread alone, but on every word that comes from the mouth of God" (Matthew 4:4). As you fill your mouth with God's Word, it will sustain your life and strengthen your relationship with Jesus Christ.

Pray Consistently. A fourth way to learn about God is through consistent prayer. Prayer is conversation with God. It doesn't have to be formal, even though that is sometimes appropriate. Often our prayer can be a simple conversation with God. The Bible has many verses dealing with prayer. For example, 1 Thessalonians 5:17 says, "Pray continually." James 5:13 says, "Is any one of you in trouble? He should pray. Is anyone happy? Let him sing songs of praise." Prayer is not something just for times of trouble. We can learn about God through different kinds of prayer. Consider these three:

Praise: Praise is thanking God and rejoicing in God's action in your life. All of life itself comes from God. What blessings have you experienced? As you list these blessings, thank and praise God.

Petition: Usually petition comes to mind first when we think of prayer. Petition is asking God to work in particular situations. We focus on the situation and discuss it with God.

Listening: In our noisy, busy world, it is sometimes hard for God to break through and get our attention. Through prayer we talk with God and try to discern His direction for our thoughts, ideas, and plans. Possibly God will direct you to a particular Bible passage while you are praying.

Prayer isn't all sitting upright with your eyes shut and your hands folded, or standing, or kneeling. Prayer can be a natural conversation taking place while you are walking through the woods or driving your car. Experiment with different forms of prayer and use these forms as another way to develop your relationship with the Lord of the Universe.

What happens if we don't pursue a personal relationship with Jesus Christ? God lets us suffer the consequences. As a nine-year-old boy, I gave my life to Jesus Christ. Reared as a preacher's son, I spent many hours in the church and had wonderful times of growing in my relationship with Christ. During this time, if another kid picked a fight with me, I simply ran away. As a result, I gained the reputation of being one of the best runners in my school! It wasn't that I was a coward; rather, I was determined to live my life as a Christian, and for me that meant not fighting.

One day three guys backed me into a place where I couldn't run away. They were slapping me around when I told them, "You'd better stop, or somebody is going to get hurt."

"Yeah," one of them sneered, "and you're that somebody, Phillip." Moments later, I swung and connected with the chin of the biggest guy. He fell down, and his friends pleaded with him, "Come on, Ballard, get up!" Ballard didn't move—he was out cold.

The boys eventually shook Ballard awake, and the three of them took off down the street. Word got out that Porter had knocked out Ballard. Almost every bully and would-be bully in town began to challenge me to fights. I was constantly getting into fights after school. One day when I was getting whipped, a guy said to me, "Porter, you'd better come down to the gym and learn how to box."

I didn't know anything about boxing, but at his encouragement I put on some gloves and learned how to box. Fighting got into my system—whether I was in the ring or on the street. From ages fourteen to nineteen, I wasn't following Jesus. I still went to church on Sundays, but I was there in body and not in heart. Besides fighting, I got involved in things such as playing cards, throwing dice, and dancing. Every day I grew more miserable because I had lost my love relationship with Jesus.

One day at age nineteen, I was sitting in church and realized how far I had wandered from God. The yearning in my heart and soul was to get back to Him. I walked down the aisle and at the altar gave my life back to God. Kenneth Copeland sings a song that says in part, "I have returned to the God of My Father, Abraham's God, the Chosen Messiah." That day I stepped back onto the path to my relationship with God.

I wish I could say that I have never wandered off that path, but I have. As a freshman in college, I was dating Lee. We met in the church and both of us loved God. Several months before our wedding, we made a big mistake and conceived our first child, Phillip. There was no question of our love for each other and our intention for marriage, so we were married in July 1957. Phillip was born in November. But we also had to confess our sin to God, accept His forgiveness, and return to the path of following Jesus. That is the Good News about our faith: God's grace is always greater than our sin.

No matter what sins you have committed in your life or what sort of holy relationship you once had with God, the important thing is to decide where you are today. God doesn't accept or reject us on the basis of holy living. I learned afresh that by His grace God accepts me just as I am. It is a daily process to learn to lean on Jesus and gradually leave our sinful ways behind.

Philippians 1:6 says, "He who began a good work in you will carry it on to completion until the day of Christ Jesus." We can be assured that attacks will often come in our spiritual lives. But we have this promise when the Bible is our standard: "A righteous man may have many troubles, but the LORD delivers him from them all" (Psalm 34:19).

My daily life is focused on following Jesus Christ and my commitment to obeying the words of God in the Bible. Such a focus keeps us on the path to purity. One of the ways we maintain this focus is the second path to purity—gathering a few brothers near us to hold us accountable.

STRAIGHT TO THE PATH

(In this chapter and the ones that follow, I have included a number of practical suggestions for living a pure and holy life. These ideas comprise this section called Straight to the Path.)

1. Are you putting first things first in your life? Consider your priorities—money, family, power, or . . . ? How can you fill the empty feelings in your life? Make a fresh commitment to honor Jesus Christ through your life.

2. I discussed four ways to learn more about God. How can you apply each of these methods in your life? Choose one of the four and begin it today—reading the Bible, studying the Bible, memorizing the Bible, or praying consistently.

3. Recall a time when you moved away from God. Do you understand the forgiving nature of God? When we step out of God's pathway, He is always waiting with open arms and forgiveness and grace for our return. Take some time to ask God to forgive you for your past and cleanse your heart of any wrongdoing.

CHAPTER THREE

DON'T GO IT ALONE

HEY, MAN, HOW TOUGH ARE YOU?" As a kid I heard that question a lot. You did, too, and in a way we are still being asked that question. The world tells us, as men, to be tough. We want to be perceived as independent and self-reliant, like the marines or the John Wayne mystique. In fact, life for most men is a constant race against some other guy. *You* know what I mean. Am I as good-looking as the guy next to me? Am I dressed as well and driving as nice a car? Am I making as much money as that fellow? Do I get promoted before he does?

At the same time, we hunger for friendship. We know we need it, but we never quite find it. If you don't think so, ask your wife. I *know* what she would say to me: "Bishop, if he had just another guy to talk to." But we don't have one. Too busy bein' a man.

While our culture whispers in our ear that we are islands, the reality is that we need other men or brothers to help us in our journey down the path to purity. Try it alone, and you'll never make it. And don't place this burden of friendship on your wife. To be the man *she* needs, you've got to find one or two men who will walk the path to purity *with* you.

I have to be honest with you. This is an area that has been very tough for me. For many years I have tried to form a men's group in my local church. We have met for different reasons such as prayer, fellowship, or Bible study. Often at a 6:00 A.M. meeting, only a few men would attend—even the lure of a sweet donut and hot coffee could not spur many to get out at that early hour. Traditionally, men's groups in most churches have amounted to a small core of men who are active in their church leadership. Regular guys seldom come out.

About the only time men in any large numbers have come together has been for sporting events. This situation radically changed with the formation of Promise Keepers. Men have filled huge stadiums across the nation with rallies. (Maybe they thought a game would break out in the stadium.) These events are great for a spiritual boost to everyday life, but what happens on Monday morning? When a man returns to his routine and workplace, does he stay as spiritual as he was at the stadium? These rallies have stirred men to have a spiritual hunger. Other men can help us keep that appetite alive.

WHY SHOULD I BE IN A GROUP?

SOON AFTER I WAS ELECTED to the board of directors of Promise Keepers, a group of men invited me to join their small group. Initially I was suspicious of the invitation and wondered, *What in the world is this all about? Why should I be a part of this small group? What are these guys after?* In fact, this group invited both of the African Americans on the board—Dick Clark and me—to join their group.

I decided to be honest: "Guys, I'm not sure if I want to be a part of your small group. I'm not sure I want to be vulnerable and transparent with you." Nevertheless, I knew a key part of keeping my commitments to purity involved an active role in such a group. Since I didn't have a group, I decided to try it for a little while. Deep down inside, I didn't have much confidence that I would be attending this group for a very long period of time. At my first meeting with these men, I said, "I want to be up front with you about my feelings. Then if you think I'm holding back for some reason, you'll know why."

They said, "That's okay. We know it takes time, and we're willing to wait and go through that process with you." Those words started a tremendous journey. I have been with this group now for three years. Our goal is to meet every week on Tuesday mornings around 8:00 A.M. We drink coffee and share what's going on in our lives.

Gradually, I learned to trust these men. We have come to know each other's families and wives along with one another's individual concerns. For my part, these men have been challenging me about my weight and about the intensity of my schedule of activities. Their honest encouragement has helped me. These men are from different businesses and denominations and even different parts of the Denver metropolitan area. Together we are learning how to be transparent in our relationships.

One of the members of our group, whom I will call Fred Joiner, learned about a year ago that his wife had cancer. "Carol" had an operation, which proved successful. During Carol's recuperation, Fred continued to meet with our group. One day he confronted us: "Hey, guys, I'm upset with you, and I'm upset with Promise Keepers. My wife has been recuperating, and no one has shown they care. No one has brought flowers or a meal or anything. I don't understand that, because you men are my close friends."

We all hung our heads in shame. We had blown it—not intentionally—even with our friends. But Fred had the freedom in our small group to express these thoughts, and we were glad he spoke up. Our busy schedules and active lives were no excuse. We had failed in our commitment to Fred and his family. It was almost Easter, so we kicked our actions into high gear.

"What do you need, Fred?" I asked. "What is something that we could get that you'd really enjoy?"

"For Easter, we've got a lot of family members coming to dinner. Carol likes ham for the holidays," Fred suggested.

"Say no more," I said. I went to a store that sells honey-baked ham and ordered a giant sliced ham, then we delivered it in the name of our group and Promise Keepers. The Joiners appreciated the gesture, but more than that, we demonstrated our interdependence and need for affirmation and love. As Carol has recuperated, she has been an active part of our lives, talking with us and making us feel like brothers and sisters.

On another morning, an attorney in the group, whom we will call Brad, brought a different concern to our meeting. He wanted our prayers and advice. "I've been struggling with an ethical situation that I need your counsel and wisdom on," Brad began. Several years ago, as a senior management partner, Brad had contracted for, purchased, and developed a piece of land. A few others had joined Brad in the business venture, but their initial investment was considerably less than his. Now the property was going to be sold at a considerable windfall, and the other partners wanted an equal share of the profits, despite their unequal investments. Brad was feeling some real pain in this situation. As a group we tried to rally around him and help him through it.

"What should I do?" he asked us. As we discussed it and prayed about God's direction in this situation, each of us felt it was a case of following the words of Jesus. In the Sermon on the Mount, Jesus said, "If someone wants to sue you and take your tunic, let him have your cloak as well. If someone forces you to go one mile, go with him two miles. . . . If you love those who love you, what reward will you get? Are not even the tax collectors doing that?" (Matthew 5:40–41, 46).

Brad didn't have to face this situation alone. He had an accountability group. He believed in us as fellow believers and built trust in our opinions. We didn't just glibly say that we would pray for him; rather, we were committed to caring about his day-to-day life.

At first I was skeptical about the purpose of this small group, but the continuity and the relationships have become important in my life. Committing oneself to such a group is not easy at first—it involves risks in slowly lowering our guard and becoming transparent. But each step has been a part of my journey along the path to purity.

IRON SHARPENING IRON

PROVERBS 27:17 SAYS, "As iron sharpens iron, so one man sharpens another." We can't go through that improvement process unless we have a friend who can talk straight with us. Even the disciples of Jesus needed to have this sharpening process in their lives.

Acts 10 relates how the apostle Peter fell into a vision about unclean animals. God told him to not call anything unclean—instead, he should go and preach to the Gentiles. In Bible times, the Jews didn't talk or associate with the Gentiles. The practice was also carried on with the early Christians, who initially were all Jewish. Then God revealed to Peter that he could go to the house of Cornelius, a Roman army officer, and preach about Jesus. After Peter and his companions told Cornelius's household about Jesus, the people there were filled with the Holy Spirit and spoke in other languages. It was obvious to Peter that God had brought salvation to all people—not just the Jewish people.

But before long, the boys from the 'hood came and convinced Peter that he wasn't a good Christian unless he kept himself within the Jewish traditions. Paul, who was also an apostle, confronted Peter about his changes in attitude and encouraged him to be true to his calling. Paul brought the great apostle Peter into an accountable relationship.

FIND THAT GROUP

WHAT ABOUT YOU? Do you have a small group of men to share your journey with? If not, give it a try. Be skeptical, just as I was.

First, try your local church. Ask your pastor for his assistance. Chances are, your church already has several small groups that would welcome you. If not, take the initiative. The next time you shake a guy's hand after church, ask him to meet you for coffee some morning. Share your desire at that time and see what happens.

Promise Keepers publishes a resource called *The Next Step*. This book details how to start a small accountability group and includes a video, audio tape, and study guide. It is available from Promise Keepers at 1–800–456–7594. You can learn more about different resources from the Promise Keeper Web page at: http://www.promisekeepers.org.

I recommend that you not have a work associate in your small group of men. Having such an associate in the group will possibly narrow what you feel comfortable discussing openly. Let's face it, men: All of us have struggles with our work, since it is a key area of life.

At the first meeting of the group and whenever someone joins, make sure everyone understands the ground rules. Even if the group has been established for a long time, it is good to go over the ground rules occasionally.

1. We're not here to talk about the weather or the latest sports events. It's fairly easy to begin a conversation with another man about the weather or sports. I consider such topics casual conversation and superficial. You can talk about these subjects in an elevator or any public location without concern.

The purpose of the group is to talk about parts of our lives in which we are struggling. Maybe you're having difficulty with your prayer life, and someone else in the group has some suggestions. Possibly you've got a difficult relationship in the workplace and need a place to air your concern. Maybe you have a family member who is troubled, and you need some help. This group of men offers a venue in which you can talk about such personal concerns. Instead of gutting it out and going it alone, you can draw on these vital relationships as a resource and a fountain of strength.

2. Confidentiality is vital to the group dynamics. It's a hard reality that some people struggle with confidentiality.

They are constantly on the lookout for fuel that can be used in the rumor mill. If you have a problem with gossip, then maybe you shouldn't be in a small group—or at least you should warn the other members. It is critical that each member realize that "what is said here stays here." This trust and confidence will be a growing factor in your relationships with these men. If the group can't be trusted to keep confidences, then ethical or moral questions or other difficulties can not be discussed. It's impossible.

3. Be sensitive to the group and make sure everyone has a chance to talk. Some of us can talk better than others in a small group. The psychologist would call this factor the difference between the extroverts and the introverts. In a small group, every person should have the opportunity to speak within the confines of the group. The amount of talking for each man will understandably ebb and flow. As one person said, "One week your seesaw is up and mine is down. Another week it is reversed and I'm down while you're up." The caution is not to let one person or one set of problems dominate the group discussion. If one person is allowed to dominate, the entire group loses its effectiveness.

4. Be committed to praying for each other. Prayer allows each man to mention a concern on his mind. I would recommend that you keep the request time short so you can spend time in prayer. Every man should take notes so he can pray for these requests in between meetings. It's a good idea to keep a small notebook especially for these requests.

Prayer is our means to touch the heart of God. The Bible tells us that God controls the hearts and minds of men—whether they acknowledge Him or not. As we pray for others, we take our focus away from our own difficulties and reach out to others. Also, as we monitor the requests and answers to prayer, we are able to thank God for his involvement in our daily lives. The time of prayer gives us another opportunity to bond and connect with the men in our small group.

ONE-ON-ONE ACCOUNTABILITY

MAYBE YOU HAVEN'T BEEN ABLE to find a group of men or you feel uncomfortable with your group. An alternative is to meet with one person on a regular basis. Follow the same rules for the group but, instead, focus on the one man.

I suggest that you meet the first time for breakfast or lunch. Give yourselves permission to talk about surface things such as sports and the weather, then move to deeper subject matter. As you meet with this person, evaluate the relationship.

Is this someone whom I enjoy meeting with?

Is this someone whom I can trust with my confidences?

Is this someone whom I can envision meeting with over a long period of time?

Will this person's schedule allow such a regular commitment?

After you answer some of these questions, you can determine if you can have one-on-one accountability with this person. You don't have to meet for a meal. It can be simply a thirty-minute time together in the middle of the day or whenever it's convenient. The important step is to find someone, if not some group, with whom you can let down your guard and share your struggles with the confidence that the other person will care and pray for you.

A friend, John Maxwell, has spoken a number of times at the Promise Keepers gatherings. He says that one of the devil's best weapons is to keep Christians from being accountable. John has an older friend named Bill with whom he meets on a regular basis for accountability. Every time they meet together, Bill asks five questions that John must answer:

1. Are you reading your Bible and praying every day?

2. Consider what's running through your mind. Are your thoughts pure?

3. Are you misusing or violating any trust that someone else has given you?

4. Are you living every day in total obedience to God? (John says that partial obedience equals disobedience.)

5. Have you lied about any of the previous questions?

You may smile at the fifth question, but consider how easy it is to stretch the truth and weasel out of being accountable. John has admitted before thousands of men at the rallies that many times he has had to stop and say, "Yeah, Bill let's go back . . ."

IT'S NOTHING NEW

YOU MAY THINK THAT THIS IDEA of a meaningful or significant relationship with another man is something new. Again, we can turn to our standard for life—the Bible—and find some insights about this concept of relationships.

Two men, Jonathan and David, had a very close relationship. They were not blood relatives, just friends. This David is the same man who was later to become king of Israel. At this time Saul was the king, and Jonathan was his oldest son. After David killed the giant Goliath, King Saul brought the young hero to his court. There David became friends with Jonathan. "Jonathan became one in spirit with David, and he loved him as himself" (1 Samuel 18:1–2).

The two young men became close friends and made a promise to support each other.

Friendship isn't always easy, and the friendship between Jonathan and David had a huge problem. As the oldest son of King Saul, Jonathan was the heir to the throne of Israel. But God had been displeased with Saul and had selected another person to be his successor—namely, David. King Saul was aware of the friendship between his son and David, but also he suspected that God had selected David as the next king. Saul tried several times to kill David, but Jonathan valued their friendship more than gaining the throne, so he warned his friend. "Jonathan said to David, 'Go in peace, for we have sworn friendship with each other in the name of the LORD, saying, "The LORD is witness between you and me, and between your descendants and my descendants forever."' Then David left, and Jonathan went back to town" (1 Samuel 20:42).

A short time later, Jonathan and Saul were killed in battle. David didn't forget his covenant of friendship. As king, David searched the kingdom for the relatives of Jonathan and found his son, Mephibosheth, and brought him into his household (2 Samuel 4:4). The bonds of such friendship go very deep into a man's heart.

A PLACE TO SHARE PAIN

A SIGNIFICANT RELATIONSHIP WITH ANOTHER MAN also gives us a place to share deep feelings. As men we tend to stuff those feelings deep inside and not let them out. We don't consider it very macho to express those feelings. But in a close friendship with another man we can release those feelings and grow in our emotional stability—instead of letting those feelings stew inside.

Through my work with Promise Keepers, I met Gordon England, a former pastor, missionary, and seminary professor, in 1992. During one of our conversations, Gordon shifted the topic from casual to serious with the question, "Have you ever experienced any pain?"

As I pondered his question, some new emotions swelled to the surface. For the first time in thirty years, I remembered the rejection of my social work application in Walsenburg, Colorado. I had buried my pain about this particular incident, but Gordon's question brought it to the surface. Suddenly, I wasn't there in a boardroom but was mentally transported back to the image of my walking out of that office when they told me I didn't have a job. Facing Gordon now, I began to choke back some tears.

Gordon put his arm around my shoulder. "Bishop, that rejection really hurt you."

"Yes," I said. Then Gordon encouraged my tears and shared that pain from my life. The experience drew us closer as brothers in Christ—and then suddenly I began to pull back. I thought, *I don't want to be this vulnerable. I've got to pull myself together.* I took my pain and shoved it back into a drawer in my heart. Maybe I wouldn't have to look at it again for another thirty years.

But Gordon sensed my need to share my experience, and he wouldn't let go of our friendship. As Gordon continued to pursue a relationship with me, I grew more and more comfortable with his friendship. I allowed myself to be more open and transparent with him. The experience has fostered a good relationship.

Gordon is one of my few white friends who feels he can drop by my house just about any time he wants to. In fact, he did arrive at my door once right around midnight for a few minutes.

When he learned that my youngest daughter, Phyllis, had been in a car accident, Gordon was concerned about her neck and back pain. The next day, Gordon telephoned Phyllis.

"I know what you must be going through, Phyllis," Gordon said. "Several years ago I had whiplash from an accident and my hot tub was exactly what I needed. Why don't you come over and use our tub?"

Phyllis listened politely but didn't accept the invitation. While I lead a relatively large congregation in Denver, our family tends to be private. "That white man wants me to come and use his hot tub," Phyllis said one day. Gordon didn't make the offer once and then forget about it. Instead, he called three or four times and encouraged Phyllis to get the help the warm water could offer. Before too long, Phyllis took advantage of this gracious offer from Gordon. It helped her neck, and maybe some other areas in her life, too.

Such a friendship between men doesn't come from just one or two attempts. Gordon is committed to my family, and I am committed to his. You can have the same kind of experience I have had. This man-to-man friendship goes beyond barriers of denomination or color. It is a critical step in our path to purity.

Unfortunately, in our world it is often difficult for men to find such relationships. Yet the second path to purity involves a commitment to pursue them. The word *pursue,* according to Webster's, means "to find or employ measures to obtain or accomplish." The task may be easy or it may be difficult, but if a man is in pursuit, he will find a means to accomplish this path to purity.

I like to compare this matter of men needing other men to a fire. If a fire runs out of fuel, it slowly dies. But if that fire is stoked with fuel and the pieces of log are kindled next to each other, they can produce a bonfire that is seen for miles and miles. In the same manner, when we pursue significant relationships with other men, our fire for living close to Jesus Christ continues to be stoked. It provides unending fuel for our search for spiritual solutions to everyday problems.

STRAIGHT TO THE PATH

1. Do you value the concept of accountability and the necessity of a vital relationship to keep on the path to purity? If you don't see the importance of this concept and fail to make it a high priority, it will be a challenge for you to keep the Promise Keepers' standard.

2. Evaluate your friendships with other men. Are there some with whom you could meet on a regular basis for accountability and developing a deep friendship? Return to the section on page 46 and follow my tips on how to find such a group. Make a commitment to take the time and energy required until you find at least one other man for a vital relationship.

3. When you meet with this other man, what happens? Prayer? Surface talk about the weather? It takes risk on your part and his to deepen the relationship. Make a commitment to go deeper. Could you use the same five questions that John Maxwell used on page 50 to move beyond casual conversation?

4. Read the story of Jonathan and David in 1 Samuel 18–20 and think about their friendship. Through pursu-

ing vital friendships with other men, we are not break-
ing new ground but continuing a tradition that
stretches back to the days of the Old Testament. Such
a friendship is a vital link in our quest for spiritual
solutions to the everyday problems of life.

CHAPTER FOUR

BEHAVE YOURSELF!

REMEMBER BACK IN JUNIOR HIGH when word came down that you would be getting "the sex talk" in P.E. class? And you got both a little nervous and a whole lot interested, but it was all pretty awkward? And to save face, you probably joked about it afterward and pretended you didn't learn a thing because you knew it all ahead of time?

Well, part of this chapter is "the sex talk." I guess we still haven't learned, because this is the area of life that causes so much trouble for so many of us. But if we are to be godly examples to our children—men of a pure and noble heart—we need to return now and then to a frank discussion of this troublesome subject.

Sex is one of four areas that require that we actually practice purity. To be a spiritual man in today's world, we need to practice sexual, spiritual, moral, and ethical purity. Admittedly, it is a challenge in a world that tells you cheating is okay—just don't get caught. And it seems as if the ethical rules for our highest government officials get bent almost daily. Let's look at each of these areas with some practical tools for maintaining pure relationships.

SEXUAL PURITY

SEXUAL TEMPTATION IS EVERYWHERE. It is in our slick magazine ads and the sensual voice in radio and television commercials. It is the attractively dressed woman in the office cubicle near our workplace. No, you certainly won't get involved with her, but you want to look—and dream. A voice whispers in your ear, "No one will know about it" or "Just this once." You'd think preachers would be immune to this, but we're not. Almost thirty-five years ago, I was a young Christian working in an Oklahoma church. Orin Boyd, an older evangelist from Wichita, Kansas, and I held a week of evangelistic meetings. A number of attractive women attended.

One day a woman we'll call Sarah, who had been at these meetings, called the church and requested that Evangelist Boyd visit her home. "I've taken ill and want Evangelist Boyd to come and pray for me," she said.

Evangelist Boyd sensed that something wasn't quite right about this request. I'm certain he heard the Persistent Voice inside saying, "It's okay. You can go and pray with Sarah. It's no problem." Instead, Evangelist Boyd heard a stronger Voice that suggested a different course of action. He asked me to accompany him on the visit.

During the drive, Evangelist Boyd told me, "Phillip, I have a bad feeling about this situation so I wanted you to come with me. I don't feel like this is an honest request."

I said, "Do you really believe this is a put-on?" The older man nodded his head. "I can feel it," he said. It didn't take long for us to reach this woman's home.

I was a few steps behind Evangelist Boyd as we walked up the sidewalk. He knocked on the screen door, then it opened. "Oh, hello!" I heard Sarah almost sing.

Suddenly Evangelist Boyd began to back away from the door, shaking his head. I caught a glimpse of Sarah wearing a small negligee. "Let's get out of here, Phillip!" Boyd said as we promptly turned around and hurried away. As we settled into our car, he said to me, "*That's* the reason I asked you to come with me."

On the path to spiritual and sexual purity, this experience became a defining moment for me. I was shocked that any woman could have such boldness about sex with a preacher, but through that experience I learned the lesson of a lifetime. Evangelist Boyd had the wisdom to sense something was wrong about the woman's request and took someone along on the visit. This Christian man knew that if it was a case of entrapment, I would stand with him for the right action.

One of the hallmarks of the Billy Graham Evangelistic Association is that Mr. Graham always travels with a companion. Throughout many years of ministry, whether on an airplane or in a hotel, Mr. Graham has made it a point not to get into situations that could even remotely be considered improper.

For men, the area of sexual purity is an enormous challenge. Most Christian men tend to deny this and pretend they are above sexual temptation. Those are usually the ones who fall. I'm the first to admit that I find women beautiful and that the way they are presented in the media makes them even more alluring. Let's not kid ourselves and think that only the *other* guy is vulnerable. The first step in keeping yourself sexually pure is to be honest with yourself and admit that it's a struggle. Here are some other strategies that have helped me deal with sexual temptation:

1. When sexual thoughts come to mind, immediately short-circuit those thoughts with something else, for if you

dwell on the thought, it opens the door to possibly following through with the fantasy. We are exhorted in Philippians 4:8, "Whatever is pure . . . think about such things." If I come across a sexy ad in a magazine, I turn my thoughts to my family and how beautiful my wife and children are. That makes it a lot easier to turn the page.

2. When you near a sexual temptation, turn and run away from it. Sam was traveling, and in the evening he walked out of the hotel. An attractive woman looked at him and said, "Honey, do you need some company tonight?"

For an instant, Sam considered the invitation, then thought about his wife and two children on the other side of the country. He said, "No, thank you. I'm full of home cooking." He closed the door to the invitation and ran away from it.

3. Replace those sexual temptations with positive acts. In almost every motel across the nation, sexually explicit movies are available for a modest fee. The previews almost lure you to watch them. But if you make a short call to the front desk, the hotel can block such films from your room. If you will be tempted to watch these films, make that call when you check into your room.

Search for ways to fill your mind with nonsexual instead of sexual thoughts. Jesus told His disciples, "The eye is the lamp of the body. If your eyes are good, your whole body will be full of light. But if your eyes are bad, your whole body will be full of darkness. If then the light within you is darkness, how great is that darkness!" (Matthew 6:22–23). Jesus is telling us that our eyes are the gateway to our mind. We need to guard the images that we store in our mind from movies, television, or any number of everyday interactions with our society. Those images are stored in our memory banks forever.

4. As you attempt to live a sexually pure life, a key principle is to have at least one spiritual brother with whom you have accountability. We dealt with this accountability relationship in the previous chapter. As a player for the Los Angeles Lakers, A. C. Green caught quite a bit of media attention for openly stating that he was a virgin. Most athletes room by themselves when they are playing on the road. But A. C. Green had a male roommate, and that was intentional. He says, "People considered it odd that a professional athlete wanted to have a roommate, but I would rather have someone around to hold me accountable. Having people covenant with me helps me to maintain a high standard." Every man needs such accountability for sexual purity—not just a professional athlete.

In the Sermon on the Mount, Jesus Christ addressed this issue of lust and sexual purity. He said, "You have heard that it was said, 'Do not commit adultery.' But I tell you that anyone who looks at a woman lustfully has already committed adultery with her in his heart" (Matthew 5:27–28).

Early in my life, I knew that I wanted to pastor a church. Pastors face three prominent pitfalls in their life's work: women, money, and liquor. I wasn't too concerned about two of these pitfalls. Our family didn't have much money, so we didn't have to worry about that aspect. Liquor and alcohol weren't available in my family and in fact was never a problem. That left women. I was determined that women would never be a problem for me. In reality, I fooled myself to think that I could be so close to God and live with such "supposed" integrity. In my fantasies, I could get into bed with a woman naked and not ever touch her. My fantasy was just that—a dream. You can't get that close to the fire in sexual temptation without being burned or falling into the trap.

Some of my friends in high school participated in "trains." They would get a girl, and several of them would have sex with this same girl in a trainlike fashion. I was invited to these "train sessions," but I turned away from any such experience. Guys would tease me, saying things such as "Phillip Porter, you never get any. Why, a good piece and a cold drink of water would kill you dead. You're so scared of women!"

As I thought about it, I puffed up with pride that I had not had sex with a woman before I married. But while I had never committed the physical sexual act, I certainly thought about sex. Jesus told His disciples that to think about sex is the same as having committed sexual intercourse. As I learned more about what God wanted for my life, I realized the foolishness of my thoughts. I repented, admitted the wrongness of my actions, and asked God's forgiveness. Now whenever these types of feelings arise, I have chosen a different path for my actions—the path of God's Word.

NO ONE WAS LOOKING—MORAL PURITY

SOME MEN HAVE LEARNED how to deal with sexual temptation, but have gotten derailed on other matters of morality. I know what I'm talking about. Like each of you, I have had my share of doing things that I knew were not right. When I was about fifteen, my father was hospitalized in Oklahoma City. As the oldest son, I had to take up my dad's janitorial work. Cleaning a local tavern was one of his regular responsibilities.

Every day I emptied trash, swept, mopped the floors, cleaned spittoons, and stacked the cases of beer. It took several hours to do this job, even when I got my two younger brothers to help me. On Friday, the owner paid me. I was shocked when he handed me the cash—fifteen dollars for seven days of hard work. I was angry and repeated, "Fifteen dollars?"

"Oh, yeah, and here's the leftover candy," the man said as he reached behind the counter and dumped some old candy bars into a small bag. "Don't you remember that your dad brought you candy?" Sure, I remembered those candy bars—but I had no idea this is where they came from. I didn't say anything else, but inside I burned with anger. In the eyes of this man, the leftover candy replaced a fair wage.

In the 1950s, such treatment was commonplace, and as a black person, I didn't dare get too verbal with my response. It might get me thrown into jail or worse. I accepted the money, yet in my heart I wanted to lash back at him.

Each day during the next week, I took a little money from the cash register. It wasn't much—just a few quarters and dimes. One morning, after we were finished, I reached into the cash register and took some change. Suddenly the manager broke out from behind several boxes.

"Caught you!" he yelled as he sprang into the room.

I threw my hands up into the air and backed away with a horrified look. His money was clutched in my hands.

"I *knew* some of my money was missing from that register! Why, I ought to throw you into jail for stealing from me, even though it's only a few quarters," he sputtered as his face turned red in anger.

"But instead of taking you to the jail, I'm going to do the next best thing," he said. "I'm going to haul you home, tell your mother, then fire you." Much to my embarrassment, that's exactly what he did.

Isn't that how we get into trouble? Just a few quarters. Just a few minutes longer on our lunch break or just a few pencils at work. Few people just decide one day to become immoral. Our commitment to high values slips a little piece at a time. I knew it was wrong to steal. As a small boy, I had been taught the Ten Commandments from the Old Testament. One of the commandments says, "You shall not steal" (Exodus 20:15). While I knew that law in my heart and knew the "right" thing to do, I turned away from it and did wrong. After all, wasn't it really "my money"—money I deserved for my hard work?

That man wronged my family with his poor payment, so in my mind I justified stealing. When we move away from God's standard, we are left to our own devices and actions. We misbehave and actually profane God's name. Proverbs 30:7–9 says,

> "Two things I ask of you, O LORD;
>   do not refuse me before I die:
> Keep falsehood and lies far from me;
>   give me neither poverty nor riches,
>   but give me only my daily bread.
> Otherwise, I may have too much and disown you
>   and say, 'Who is the LORD?'
> Or I may become poor and steal,
>   and so dishonor the name of my God."

Because of your commitment to honoring Jesus Christ, you naturally do not want to profane God's name with any questionable immoral actions. That means we take care of the little things before they become big things. Amen?

SPIRITUAL PURITY

DURING THE EARLY 1980S, I faced an unusual temptation. Representatives of the Unification Church invited me to a luncheon. Founded by the Reverend Sun Myung Moon, this large church movement is based in Korea. The leader of the luncheon was a young pastor whom I had known for a number of years when he was preaching the Good News about Jesus Christ and singing His praises in church. But this pastor had gone into the Unification Church and now was recruiting for the Reverend Moon.

I had studied the Unification Church and concluded that this group had founded its beliefs and doctrine not on the Bible but on the opinion of a single man—Reverend Moon. In my mind, the Unification Church was a cult—and that's when my spiritual temptation came into the picture.

At this luncheon Moon's associates were recruiting a large number of pastors—black and white. They offered everyone there an opportunity to take an all-expenses-paid trip to Korea. Moon wanted us to come and see his work firsthand. There were other incentives for making the trip. While we were in Korea we could visit the church of David Yonggi Cho, the well-known Pentecostal pastor who leads the largest church in the world. We could obtain tailored suits—not a small consideration by any means. I'm a pretty big guy and have always found it a challenge to find well-made suits for my work as a pastor. In Korea, these tailor-made suits could be purchased quite inexpensively. Talk about a temptation! At that time, I had never traveled outside the United States. A number of my pastor-friends knew that the Unification Church was a cult, but they still accepted their invitation to go overseas—mostly for the suits.

As I prayed about this opportunity, I felt that if I went, I would be letting down my spiritual and ethical guard. Part of the agenda for the Korea trip required taking different seminars taught by the Unification Church and listening to their false teaching. I told my recruiting pastor-friend, "I don't want to go to Korea."

He asked, "Why? If you go, it doesn't mean that you're a 'Moonie.' It just means that as Christians we're showing unification."

I shook my head. "No, I don't ever want it to be said that Phillip Porter ever gave this man the time of day." It was a tough call, but I was resolved not to give Reverend Moon any portion of my allegiance or mind.

To my amazement, a number of Christian pastors from the Denver area and elsewhere in the United States agreed to take this trip. I felt I understood that to move onto the devil's territory dishonors the lordship of Jesus Christ. To my way of thinking, to take this trip would have been a violation of my integrity and standards. Others apparently felt they could flirt with the devil yet not be burned in the fires of temptation. But I don't think such flirting is possible without compromising your integrity.

Because—*I* think it was because—I did not compromise my spirituality, years later God provided another chance for me to have a tailored suit, under a different set of circumstances. As the chairman of the board of Promise Keepers, I traveled to India in 1996 along with Coach Bill McCartney and a number of other men. There, at the insistence of the local Christians, I was fitted for a beautiful tailor-made suit.

ETHICAL PURITY

EVERY YEAR AROUND APRIL 15 I am confronted with an ethical question: Do I follow the rules for reporting my income, or do I bend them a little so I don't have to pay so much tax? Maybe *you* enjoy a bit of gambling this time of year—

playing the odds to see if your return will escape an Internal Revenue Service audit. Again you can hear the Persistent Voice: "Just do it. You won't get caught."

In ethical affairs, as in moral, spiritual, and sexual matters, we must know our standard. Do you have a firm standard for integrity? Or are you tossed in the winds of change? If you don't have some guiding principles for your life, then you fall for anything.

The book of James discloses the source of wisdom, then tells us what to do when doubts come into our minds: "If any of you lacks wisdom, he should ask God, who gives generously to all without finding fault, and it will be given to him. But when he asks, he must believe and not doubt, because he who doubts is like a wave of the sea, blown and tossed by the wind. That man should not think he will receive anything from the Lord; he is a double-minded man, unstable in all he does" (James 1:5–8). I love this image of the tossing sea. Isn't that exactly like a man with doubts? We are tossed around and pulled in every direction by the dissonant claims and messages we hear out in the world. I want my beliefs and day-to-day activities to be based firmly on the truth from the Bible.

You see, ethics is simply the acting out of our beliefs. If you say you are a Christian and that you believe the Bible, your actions will show it. That is why I have a hard time with Christian men who are known for their ability to tell a coarse, dirty joke. I know we're all just a bunch of guys and that some of those jokes really are funny—but does this behavior truly reflect what we believe?

This is a matter in which you have an awesome responsibility to your children. By your actions you are teaching them how to live. Again, it is the little things that often speak the loudest. If the cashier undercharges you, do you gloat about it once you get in the car, or do you go back and make it right? If the sign says, KIDS 12 AND UNDER EAT FREE, do you tell your thirteen-year-old to keep his mouth shut? Do you get a laugh at home by mimicking minorities or telling "Polack jokes"?

Men, step up to the challenge. Set high standards for yourself. Be a beacon of light to your family, your neighbors, your fellow believers.

WHEN TEMPTATION COMES

NO ONE IS PERFECT when it comes to these four areas of purity—sexual, moral, ethical, and spiritual. Romans 3:23 tells us that "all have sinned and fall short of the glory of God." All of us fail at times—and every day we are tempted to fail. I fail more than I like to admit, so here are some things I have learned that help me overcome temptation.

Build a Relationship. The problem with relationships is the cost. Wow, are they expensive! They call for complete honesty with the other person. Deep relationships with other people can help you move toward a greater degree of integrity in your life. If you have this kind of relationship, you can go to your friend and say, "I'm having a bad day. I'm really angry with myself and the situations around me. I don't know what to do. I really want to make this money because I'm not making it in my business or not being paid what I think I'm worth. This new venture will set our family in a position where we will not be in a begging mode of living."

Each of us needs to develop friends whom we can count on for their counsel and advice. These friends will recognize your needs or "success syndrome" and honestly tell you their opinion. They will ask key questions such as, What is your motive for the plan you have in mind? Is it success for the sake of success, or is it based on need? The Bible tells us that "for lack of guidance a nation falls, but many advisers make victory sure" (Proverbs 11:14). As we gather wise advisers or counselors around us, we can make good decisions and have victory in our lives.

Make No Snap Decisions. The old saying has some truth: Haste makes waste. I often come to regret it whenever I am rushed into a particular situation. If the decision is minor, the consequences are minimal. But for the major decisions of life such as career, marriage, or family, giving some time for consideration will not hinder the decision or have negative consequences. The Bible repeatedly tells us the value of patience: "Through patience, you gain possession of your soul" (see Luke 21:19), and "they that wait upon the LORD shall renew their strength; they shall mount up with wings as eagles; they shall run, and not be weary; and they shall walk, and not faint" (Isaiah 40:31 KJV).

There is great value in waiting for direction, then moving with certainty. That is not to say that we can never take advantage of opportunity when it knocks on the spur of the moment. If we live each day in a right relationship with the Lord of the Universe, we will be ready when these opportunities come our way.

I recounted earlier the occasion when Coach McCartney and other representatives from Promise Keepers approached me about my becoming a member of the board. You will recall that I told them, "The right thing to do is to honor the community and to be men of integrity about representing the African American community. You need to go to those spokespersons for the community and the Ministerial Alliance, then present your case to them and see if we are selected to serve. They need to have a say in this decision."

The men from Promise Keepers agreed with this approach, saying, "If this is the way you make your decisions, then we need to fit into this system."

When I turned this decision over to the Ministerial Alliance, I was not assured that I would get the position. I was not a popular leader among this group, yet I knew it was the right thing to place the decision in their hands. If the decision didn't stand the testing and scrutiny of the Ministerial Alliance, God was not calling me to be on the Promise Keepers board of directors.

We have to allow quiet time in the midst of our busy schedules so we can turn to God during the peaks and valleys of life's experiences. These valleys and peaks are inevitable. If we insist on going at full speed, we rush blindly ahead without God's help and guidance. We reach canyons and dead-ends that would not have concerned us if we had checked out the land ahead of time. We would have been better prepared to face the giants that could be lurking there unseen.

Taking time out was important to the Lord Jesus when He walked the earth. The crowds pursued Him. These people wanted to touch Jesus and experience His healing power or listen to His teaching and relish the way He shook the religious leaders in His day. Yet, as we read in Mark 1:35, after one of His busiest days, Jesus got up early in the morning and went out to pray. Indeed, it was His custom to slip away every day in order to talk with His heavenly Father.

In the same way, we need to steal time from our daily schedule to talk with our heavenly Father.

Draw from the Source of Strength. I found that my belief in the Bible was the key to changing my thinking. The natural reaction is not to turn to the Bible as the absolute means of truth and guidance. In our pride we think, *There must be another way.* Often we turn inward to ourselves. We feel we must have the inner strength to handle our thought lives. Yet when we try, we fail.

Or we turn to the philosophies of the world. We listen to "infomercials" or the get-rich-quick schemes around us. "This must be the way of strength," we decide. We pursue riches and fame and fortune. Yet we learn that none of these bring happiness or produce the results we hoped for.

Or I may turn to the traditions of the world: Hard work and industry will bring success. I put in long hours with my business and therefore neglect my family. I study hard and earn degrees as a means to get ahead. Yet when I talk with men who have tried this route without God, their lives have ended up empty and shallow.

The only means that I have discovered to walk in purity is to have a day-to-day relationship with Jesus Christ through reading God's Word and applying it carefully to my daily life. It is indeed a day-to-day process.

Deuteronomy 28:1–2 promises us, "If you fully obey the LORD your God and carefully follow all his commands I give you today, the LORD your God will set you high above all the nations on earth. All these blessings will come upon you and accompany you if you obey the LORD your God." Obedience is the key if we are to experience God's direction and blessing. The path to purity is an everyday process and a growing experience. We never arrive at perfection in our relationship to God, but each day we grow deeper in it as we walk in obedience.

Listen to God's Voice. Each of us has been created with a conscience. When we listen to this still, small voice, we can discern whether we are headed into trouble or freedom. Sadly, many people ignore their conscience and stumble down the road. If we repeatedly ignore this voice, it will finally quit speaking. The Bible talks about someone in this state as having a "seared conscience." That person has turned off his still, small voice of integrity.

Over the years, I have gained a great deal of strength and encouragement from the words in Isaiah 26:3: "You will keep in perfect peace him whose mind is steadfast, because he trusts in you." It is only as we keep our minds centered in God and the Bible that we are able to summon peace for every situation. You can begin on a small scale. Maybe you need to take five minutes every lunch hour for a time of prayer. After you have managed five minutes, increase it to ten minutes of prayer and ten minutes of reading from the Bible. Don't expect to become a spiritually sensitive man in an instant, but take steps each day to grow in your spiritual connection and knowledge of God on your path to purity.

Each day seek to create a consistent awareness of God's presence in your life. Even if you are all by yourself in a room, you are not actually alone. God's presence is in the room whether or not you consciously acknowledge that presence. No action can separate us from God's love; it is ever present. Romans 8:38–39 says, "For I am convinced that neither death nor life, neither angels nor demons, neither the present nor the future, nor any powers, neither height nor depth, nor anything else in all creation, will be able to separate us from the love of God that is in Christ Jesus our Lord."

Take a minute to read that verse from your Bible. Think about each section and consider how none of the things mentioned can separate you from God's love.

As men we have a responsibility to seek a spiritual solution to the difficulties of sexual, moral, ethical, and spiritual temptations. We need to focus on God's voice and His Word, the Bible. Finally, avoid or flee situations in which you could be compromised. When we are focused on God's direction, we will hear His voice and be able to stand strong against temptation and failure.

STRAIGHT TO THE PATH

1. Recommit yourself to following the Bible day by day on the path to purity. In the split second that you need to make decisions regarding sexual, moral, ethical, or spiritual matters, ask yourself, "What would Jesus do?" Then follow that guidance.

2. Fortify your resolve and commitment to purity by learning some verses of strength from the Bible such as Jeremiah 29:13; Psalm 51:10; and Jeremiah 33:3.

3. Risk the honest discussion of moral issues with another man or with your accountability group. Before the meeting, think of different areas where you have struggled to behave yourself. Then have the courage to talk about these experiences with this man or group, and ask for their assistance so you can stay on the right path.

4. Consider some experiences when you violated God's plans for sexual, ethical, moral, or spiritual purity. Are you still living with the guilt arising from these

actions, or have you sought God's forgiveness? No sin is too great that God cannot handle it. Jesus Christ came to earth for the forgiveness of sins. Take these matters to God in prayer and make a fresh commitment to take steps of true repentance (that is, turn from the past and not return to it again).

CHAPTER FIVE

BE THE GUARDIAN OF YOUR HOME

THE FEAR EVERY MAN HAS FELL on John Perkins. His career in the California grocery business was growing fast, and John reveled in it. With his wife, Vera Mae, John had moved from the cotton fields of Mississippi to reap higher wages in southern California. Then one day Vera Mae announced, "I'm leaving, John. I'm packing my bags and moving back to Mississippi." It was more than a threat, and soon John was alone.

Although John didn't know it, Vera Mae was two months pregnant with their first child, Spencer. Ten months after Spencer's birth, Vera Mae decided to give their marriage another try. This time it stuck. For the last forty years, John and Vera Mae have been almost inseparable.

Not every marriage has such a happy ending. Thousands of marriages have crumbled in the United States. Sometimes you can see that crumbling beginning to take place. Maybe you are absorbed in your career to the point that you neglect your family. At other times you think your marriage is on a normal keel—maybe not extremely close, but still normal—then wham! The words hit you in the face: "I can't take it any more. I'm leaving."

If we are ever to live pure lives before God, we have to follow the fourth path to purity by guarding our marriage and families. Men, to see the problems in American society, most of us don't have to go any farther than stepping out our front doors—or maybe we can even just see from inside. In many families, Dad took off and Mom is struggling to raise the children on her own. Dad didn't want the responsibility of raising children, so when he found out his woman was pregnant, he disappeared. Many mothers are living on welfare to raise their children because their husbands aren't around.

America is facing huge social problems, and we can't look to the government for solutions. Instead, we need to seek a spiritual solution to this everyday problem. Let's admit it, men: We have not protected our homes and guarded them properly. Because men have not honored their wedding vows to "love, cherish, and protect" their wives, many communities have fallen apart. We men have not been available when our teenage sons have shown the first sign of joining a gang. Indeed, the gangs are but one more system that has sprung up to fill the void for teens in fatherless homes. Is it any wonder that these teens don't know how to act like men and become the guardians of their families?

Possibly you are one of these men who doesn't know his father. You have lost the example, or role model, of someone to bond with and learn from. You have felt a spiritual drought in your life. You are asking important questions such as, How do I treat a woman? How do I be a father to my children? Those of you who have attended a Promise Keepers rally have seen something stirring in American society. I have seen it in your faces as your lives have been touched with fresh awareness of your responsibilities at home.

As we follow this fourth path to purity, I hope you will renew your commitment to your marriage and family. Vow to protect and love them with new instruction from God's Word.

HOW TO BUILD A STRONG MARRIAGE

MY INTERNAL ALARM SOUNDED—4:30 A.M. Before I got out of bed, I prayed for my wife, Lee, and laid my hands on her head. I didn't invent this pattern of prayer for my wife, but learned it from my friend, Coach McCartney. Several years ago, Coach demonstrated at one of the large Promise Keepers gatherings how he prays for his wife. I have adopted the practice.

As I was praying for Lee, I heard the still, small voice of God saying, "This is your greatest investment." The words caught me by surprise. I thought, *Wow!* I immediately thought of some other great investments in my life: my eight children, my soul.

Then the Lord said, "I know about those other investments, but I've given you your wife so that with her and through her, you can make your greatest investment."

God reminded me that before I had invested in anything else—home, car, stocks and bonds—He had given me my wife, Lee. We have been married about forty years. Lee and I have been involved in starting a small church in the Denver area. It takes a tremendous effort to officiate at weddings and funerals, counsel hurting people, and attract new people to the church. I have become involved in community

activities such as the Colorado Civil Rights Commission and
the local Parent-Teacher Association. Each of these activities
and investments are good in and of themselves, but my
greatest investment is my wife.

It takes proper care to reap increased returns on our
investments. A profitable investment doesn't come by hap-
penstance or accident, but through careful monitoring of
the circumstances.

Possibly you have been like me and have tended to
ignore and underestimate this important investment—your
wife. Maybe you have tucked your funds into a savings
account and have almost forgotten their existence, assum-
ing that the interest would compound daily, weekly, and
annually without any additional effort.

As I lay in bed early in the morning with my arms
wrapped around Lee, I could hear God's voice again: "How
well have you invested up until now? In her mind? In her
body? In her soul?"

Lee and I have more children than most of the people
around us. I thought we would get our personal returns
from our eight children—through their lives and what they
do and accomplish for society, plus through their own children, our grandchildren. But the Lord said to me, "Not so,
your *greatest* investment is your wife."

Over the years I have not always treated Lee as my greatest asset, and as a result I have not collected the best yield
from my investment. That morning, the Lord challenged me
to invest in three areas of my wife's life—her mind, her
body, and her soul. I challenge you to consider these kinds
of investments in your wife.

Investment in Her Mind. I tend to be the more vocal and
outspoken partner in our marriage. Lee is reserved and

quiet. But I have learned to listen to her and make sure that I hear her heartbeat. This is part of investing in her mind.

Recently I was scheduled to speak about "investing in your family" before 51,000 men at the Denver Promise Keepers meeting. On that Friday afternoon I was eager to get to the hotel and then to Mile High Stadium in preparation for the opening session. We were entertaining Henry Mallory, a pastor from South Africa, in our home, and he was planning to attend the conference with me.

For a few minutes, I waited—impatiently—for my wife. I paced the floor at our house, flipped through some news magazines on a table, and looked at my watch every few minutes. Henry simply sat and watched me fidget. Finally I couldn't stand it any more and called upstairs to Lee. She *still* wasn't ready. "Baby, Henry and I need to leave for the conference. We'll meet you at the hotel.'"

"All right, dear," she called back. We left and got into my car.

Pastor Henry is a soft-spoken man of medium build— a bit of a contrast with me. His first language is Afrikaans, and he speaks English with a British accent. As we drove toward downtown Denver, Henry turned to me and asked, "Now, Bishop Porter, what are you talking to the men about this weekend? I thought it was something about your greatest investment. It looks to me like we just left your greatest investment back at your house."

His words cut straight to my heart. "You're right, Henry, I need to do something about this mistake."

I reached for my cellular telephone and dialed my home number. Lee answered the phone and said she was almost ready. I told her, "We'll be back home for you in a few minutes." I turned the car around and arrived at home just as

Lee was ready to leave. My greatest investment and I went to the meeting together.

When we make a mistake in a relationship, we need to take immediate action to correct it. Sometimes pride gets in the way, and we tend to say, "I'll handle it later" or "I'll talk with her about it when I get back home." In the rush of life, we brush the mistake under a giant emotional rug. One day, the dust will pile into a huge hump under the rug and cause us to trip and fall—if we don't handle the small things of a relationship. The apostle Paul wrote in Ephesians 4:26–27: "'In your anger, do not sin': Do not let the sun go down while you are still angry, and do not give the devil a foothold." Unfortunately, many times we sweep the dust of our anger under a rug. Watch out, because someday you will trip and smash your face on these built-up feelings.

Through the years, I have validated Lee's mind because she is my sounding board. More than that, she challenges my perspectives and opinions. Long ago I told her, "Lee, you don't talk much, and I tend to talk a lot. You need to talk more and challenge me." Many times her challenge comes in her silence because what she does not say can drive me crazy.

For example, after a Sunday morning service, I try to determine from Lee if my sermon hit home with the people. I spend many hours preparing a sermon that I believe will meet the spiritual needs of my church. But I wait for feedback from Lee. How did the message go over with the people? In my mind, if the highest score were a hundred and the lowest score zero, I would believe I had scored a hundred. As we drive home from church, Lee is talking about everything but my sermon. She's pointing out something on the landscape. Or she's talking about who was or was not at church. She's discussing what we will eat for dinner or telling some story about one of our children. Inside, I'm dying to hear Lee's opinion of my sermon. I want to hear Lee say, "You did a masterpiece in your message today." Instead, she continues to talk about everything else.

I wait.

And I wait.

And I continue to wait until I can't stand it any longer. At last I say, "Lee, how did I do with the message today?"

In the early years, this question was greeted with a long pause, then finally: "Dad, I keep telling you that you preach over the folks' heads. You need to preach to their hearts. You use too many big words. You didn't bring the concept to a practical level." Like darts from the hand of a master dart thrower, her words and thoughts hit home in my heart. I would shake my head and say, "You're right." She talks to me about these important concepts and gives me feedback.

Over the years I have invested in her mind with this type of interaction. I have invested in her self-esteem. She has the ability to cut to the heart of the issue and confront me—someone who is comfortable speaking to hundreds of people. Lee continues to challenge me about the content of my messages and gently encourage me to make my sermons more practical.

Are you investing in your wife's mind? In many practical matters, our wives can challenge us and strengthen our marriage.

1. Take the time to listen to your wife—every day. Maybe you're listening with one ear and the other part of your brain is reading the newspaper or watching a baseball game. Turn off that television set or radio and give your wife your full attention.

2. Encourage your wife's intellectual development. In many Christian homes, the man got his education while his wife worked to put him through. That doesn't mean she didn't want to learn. She may be interested in taking a class at the local college or adult education program. Try to take a course together, or if you can't because of the children, volunteer to baby-sit so your wife can attend. Or there may be a seminar or Bible study that your wife would like to attend. Do more than encourage her involvement; afterward, let her tell you what she's learned from the experience. Allowing her to talk about such matters will crystallize the teaching in her own life and also give you an additional bonding point with your mate.

3. Discuss world and local affairs with your wife. Don't just limit discussion to your co-worker at the office or your buddy next door. Possibly because of her caring for the children or other duties in the home, your wife doesn't have as much time as you to listen to the news or read the newspaper. Make sure she receives the intellectual stimulation from you of discussing what's happening in the world.

4. Beyond world affairs, challenge your wife's spiritual development. Make time to read the Bible together or simply talk about the sermons you hear in church. What points have made a difference in her life? What impact did the message have on your life? As you discuss spiritual matters, you will be strengthening the application of God's truth in her daily living.

Beyond the Mind—Her Body. Besides mental stimulation, we need to invest in our wives' bodies. When was the last time you stood back from your wife and appreciated or acknowledged her beauty? As men, we need to dress our wives like queens, then validate their appearance with a compliment so they know that they have our complete attention.

Speaking of your attention, when another woman passes by and you're with your wife, where do your eyes turn? How do you honor your wife? Do you stare after the beautiful woman and collect a disgusting look from your wife? Or do you turn to your wife and start a conversation, fixing your eyes on her? In every situation, large and small, we need to invest in our wives' bodies.

Besides guarding our eyes, men, we need to encourage our wives toward a healthy lifestyle. Lee and I recently visited a health clinic in California. The staff evaluated our eating habits, weight, and exercise regimen. Then the clinic developed a program so we can have a more healthful lifestyle. You may not need to tackle anything so drastic, but consider how you are investing in your wife's health. First, are you taking care of your own health so you will be physically able to take care of your wife. Too many men put on the pounds while their wives work hard to keep their weight down. Next, are you encouraging your wife toward exercise and healthful eating habits? Exercise and eating are two important matters to consider as we invest in our wives.

The apostle Paul had much to say about husbands investing in their wives. Ephesians 5:25–28, 33 says,

> Husbands, love your wives, just as Christ loved the church and gave himself up for her to make her holy, cleansing her by the washing with water through the word, and to present her to himself as a radiant church, without stain or wrinkle or any other blemish, but holy and blameless. In the same way, husbands ought to love their wives as their own

bodies. . . . However, each one of you also must love his wife as he loves himself, and the wife must respect her husband.

What exactly does Paul mean in this passage? It could say, "Husbands, I want you to love your wives. If you want to know how to do that, ask Christ, because He loved the church." Depending on the punctuation in a particular translation, verse 25 could mean, "Husbands, love your wives, as Christ the Savior of the body loved the church," or it could mean, "Husbands, love your wives, as Christ was the savior of the body and therefore you are the savior of your wife's body." You are the protector, or rescuer, of your wife's body in the sense of helping her realize her full potential.

In addition, Paul clearly gives husbands the responsibility of guarding the marriage. First Corinthians 7:4 says, "The husband's body does not belong to him alone but also to his wife." Then, "the wife's body does not belong to her alone but also to her husband."

Often we men look around for role models about treating our wives. Then we fall into a cultural trap that says, "Be the man! Don't wash those dishes or cook any meals. That's woman's work!"

As men, we tend to take our cues from the latest movie or television program. On the large or small screen, we watch men strut their stuff and generally mistreat their wives. Or we like to follow the sports figures. Unfortunately, judging from the newspapers, a few of our "heroes" haven't turned into good role models. Many Hollywood marriages crumble in divorce court after a few months or years. Our sports heroes get hooked on drugs or alcohol or women. It is dangerous to make another man your role model for a good husband or father. These human, flesh and blood examples are too prone to failure and weakness.

We need to turn, instead, to the greatest servant in the history of mankind—Jesus Christ. His life and example should teach us how to love our wives. While Jesus Christ was never married, He showed His compassion and concern for family situations. For example, in Nain, Jesus happened on the funeral of the only son of a widow. Jesus' heart went out to the widow, and He said to her, "Don't cry." Then He raised this man from the dead (Luke 7:11–17). Also, when Jesus hung on the cross at Calvary, He took the time to present His mother to John and asked that John care for His mother (John 19:26–27). In spite of His agony in dying, Jesus took up a family matter with dignity. Through the sacrificial death of Jesus' body, Christ saved the body of the church. In the same way, as men we need to save the body of our marriage.

We are charged to take the most earnest care of our wives' bodies—to be concerned that we meet her deepest needs—emotionally and sexually. Early in my marriage, I discovered that I was no Casanova. Raised in a strong and strict home, we did not talk about having sex—whether before or after marriage. The subject never came up in conversation. When I was a boy, Dad took me aside and said, "Young man, you be careful about your body and don't go out here and get any of these young girls pregnant. Because if you do, you've got to marry them." This brief caution amounted to my total sex education from my father.

Lee and I married, and after about four children, I realized that I was no super lover. About this time I was concerned that I meet the deepest needs of my wife—physically as well as emotionally. Inside, I sensed an unexpressed longing in my marriage so I tried to get some answers and insight into this need in my wife. I began with prayer and asked God for His wisdom and insight. One of the wisest men who walked the face of the earth was King Solomon. In Ecclesiastes 2:26, Solomon wrote, "To the man who pleases him, God gives wisdom, knowledge and happiness, but to the sinner he gives the task of gathering and storing up wealth to hand it over to the one who pleases God." Beyond turning to God, I also sought the advice of some older men who loved God, and I also received some wise counsel in a couple of Christian books.

Marriage is more than someone to live with and have sex with. We need to be intimate with our wives. Intimacy is really "into-me-see." As we see into the other person, what are *her* thoughts, *her* needs, *her* concerns? We live in a "me"-centered world. "If it feels right, then do it," says one commercial. But a life that follows the standard of the Bible is focused on other people and their needs. Every day we need to work at meeting our wives' needs for intimacy.

I have learned that happiness in bed has a strong connection to my interactions with my wife earlier that day or earlier in the week. You need to make the time to

- Compliment your wife
- Express appreciation for her meals
- Comment on her beauty, patience, or anything else that serves to raise her opinion of herself
- Call her during a workday and talk about her activities (especially if you are away from home)
- Share responsibility for the children—such as taking them to their sports activities, the doctor, or school

Each of these activities with your wife is important, but the overall cumulation is greater than the sum of the parts and will have a lasting effect on strengthening your marriage. Pillsbury has an old slogan, "Nothing says loving like something from the oven, Pillsbury says it best." If I come home and smell the pie or the cake coming from the oven, I know that I have really scored in the intimacy area in recent days. I also know that when we close the bedroom door at night, we are going to experience a little bit of heaven on earth. The start of such action begins hours earlier as I reach out to meet her deepest needs.

Perhaps there would be less business for the massage parlors of America if husbands and wives became the masseurs to their mates. We would learn about sharing and caring for the body.

In America, the perfume business is a multimillion-dollar enterprise and for good reason. Consider the scents that you enjoy on your wife. What types of fragrances does she enjoy? Make a point to know this and then buy what she likes. As you learn to delight in her fragrance and the sweetness of her smell, you will draw closer as a couple. It is part of investing in her body.

As we make these investments in our own bodies and our wives', we will develop long-lasting bonds for our marriage relationship and strengthen our family life. The process isn't simple or a one-time event, but takes a daily and continual effort for a lasting impact.

Investment in Her Soul. It's easy for us to consider the mind and the body, but many of us have neglected to invest in the soul of our wives. What time do we take to study God's Word together? What time do we take to allow our spouse to explain the Scriptures to us?

Consider how your wife expresses herself spiritually. Is it through singing, or teaching, or serving as a role model for younger women? Discover what means your wife uses, then encourage her to express herself spiritually. Maybe you can offer to watch the children while she goes to choir practice or teaches a Bible study. Possibly you will need to give her the opportunity to meet with another woman one on one so she can be a role model and example. Make a conscious effort to invest in her soul.

How well do you pray together? Perhaps my greatest intimacy with my wife occurs during prayer. In our times of prayer Lee can see my struggles, hurts, pain, and tears. She can also experience my joys, expectations, and hopes for the future. In prayer I can reveal my most personal side to my wife, and she likewise to me. When we reveal our inner selves, we are really saying to our wives, "Be intimate with me. See my struggles. See my hurts and pains. Experience my fears and know my joys, expectations, and hopes. Understand the urging of my being."

Usually my most intimate moments with Lee occur early in the morning when I place my hand on her head and pray. This time is free of any distractions—no phones or interruptions. Instead, there is a deep connection of my spirit to God in the company of my wife.

BE THE GUARDIAN OF YOUR FAMILY

IN ADDITION TO CARING FOR OUR WIVES, if we are to follow this path to purity, we also need to be the guardian of the home—to love and protect and teach biblical values. Several years ago, my brother Michael took a job that required traveling two or three weeks out of the month. Michael and his wife had several small children. One day my brother received a wake-up call from his oldest son. This boy told Michael, "It doesn't seem like we have a dad anymore." Those few words struck like a spear into Michael's heart. He immediately decided to quit that position and search for another. His choice was costly for his family; he searched several months before he found another job. Michael could have passed off his son's brief comment as unimportant. Instead, he took immediate action to change the course of his career. He took up the cause to invest in his marriage and family.

The apostle Paul wrote to his friend and protégé Timothy about the qualifications for elders and deacons in the church. Although these instructions apply specifically to these two offices, they more generally give us some worthwhile guidelines for living as husbands and fathers. Let's examine some of these qualifications as husbands. "Now the overseer [elder] must be above reproach, the husband of but one wife, temperate, self-controlled, respectable, hospitable, able to teach, not given to drunkenness, not violent but gentle, not quarrelsome, not a lover of money" (1 Timothy 3:2–3). Take a few minutes to examine each of these qualities against your own life:

- Above reproach
- Temperate and self-controlled
- Respectable
- Hospitable
- Able to teach
- Not given to drunkenness (or any other substance that puts us out of control)
- Not violent but gentle (how many of us have a problem with anger?)
- Not quarrelsome (not prone to arguing)
- Not a lover of money (keeping priorities straight in life)

Each of these qualities is important to being a godly husband and father.

Paul has more instruction: "He [the elder] must manage his own family well and see that his children obey him with proper respect. (If anyone does not know how to manage his own family, how can he take care of God's church?)" (vv. 4–5). We may be excellent businessmen or managers in the workplace, but how well are we doing at home? Husbands who place a high priority on their homes and spending time with their children will have their respect and obedience.

Paul applies many of the same credentials and qualifications to the office of deacon. The point is that fathers and husbands have a high calling, and it will take a large investment on our part to be successful in the home.

MY SHARE OF MISTAKES

As a pastor I have made my share of mistakes. Several years ago, my second son, Steve, tried out for the high school football team. The school was located near our church in West Denver. On the fateful day, Steve could hardly wait to get out of his football clothes and run over to tell Dad that he had made the team.

When Steve arrived, he proclaimed with great excitement, "Dad, I made the team!"

I turned and said, "Yeah, but are you starting?" Steve walked away crushed and thought, *Daddy, you didn't hear what I said. I made the team!* At the time, Steve was a junior in high school, and I just assumed that he would make the team. We tend to ascribe success to our children, and if they don't measure up to *our* standard, we don't affirm them properly. I was so preoccupied with my duties at the church that I didn't take the time to understand what was important to Steve. Sometimes my own priorities interfered with my duties as a father.

As fathers, we need to take time to find out what's important to our children and then make those things our priority and focus.

Here are five principles that will help us become better guardians of our children:

1. *Just Be There.* The apostle Paul compares his ministry to fatherhood and instructs us accordingly: "We dealt with each of you as a father deals with his own children, encouraging, comforting and urging you to live lives worthy of God, who calls you into his kingdom and glory" (1 Thessalonians 2:11–12). None of these qualities will transpire unless the father is in the house. He can't be going here, there, and everywhere. When your children are lying down to sleep or waking up or headed off to school, it is important to be there. Make sure you attend their sporting events or drama presentations—whatever is important to them—even though it may mean making a sacrifice and giving up something else you would like to do. Also, we need to take time to pray with our children on a regular basis. We can't do it if we're not with them. Sometimes this prayer will take place at home, and sometimes in the car or just before they enter the school doors or the workplace— but it has to happen somewhere.

2. *Be Loyal.* Children need the foundation stone of a father in their lives. They find in their father's life a guide and anchor as they grow and look to the future. My children have told me, "We know you're our dad and that you won't leave us or forsake us. We can count on you."

One day I told my second daughter, "I want to thank you, Denise, for being a very careful young woman. You have brought no shame on your mom or me by being indiscreet."

Without missing a beat, Denise replied, "Yes, Dad, and I want to thank you, too, for not bringing shame on me or the family." Loyalty runs deep and is a critical and often neglected aspect of fatherhood.

3. *Love Their Mother.* My children know beyond any doubt that I love their mother deeply. We are reserved about our display of affection, but we express it often in front of them. Do you honor your wife by opening doors for her or sharing money with her? Is she confident that in your relationship you are equals? While the answers to these questions may not be voiced by your children, they will implicitly know them from the way you treat your wife.

Your openly displaying love toward your wife will help your children have greater security in these days of disintegrating families and rampant divorce. A father's love for his children is often reflected in the way he honors his wife.

4. *Just Be Daddy or Poppy or Dad.* My oldest daughter once stopped by one of the meetings of the board of directors of Promise Keepers and stuck her head in the door. The chemistry between us was obvious to everyone in the room. I introduced Katherine to the board, and she called me "Poppy"! Immediately someone said to me, "Now we see where you get your good looks!" No matter what title or position I may hold in my church or denomination or another group such as Promise Keepers, there is nothing quite as important or heartwarming as being called "Dad"— or in this case, "Poppy."

5. *Share Your History with Your Children.* Until a few years ago, I took many of my growing-up experiences for granted. Those were difficult years, and America has gone through many changes since those days of de facto segregation and Jim Crow laws. Because of the pain I suffered in those experiences, I hid them from my children and made no effort to talk about them. That left a vacuum in their lives that my stories could have filled. When I talk about those early years, my children gain strength to know that when they experience tough times in their lives, they too can come through them with victory in Jesus.

The prophetic words of Malachi 4:6 challenge us to follow these guiding principles for godly fatherhood: "He will turn the hearts of the fathers to their children, and the hearts of the children to their fathers." These principles offer some significant solutions to everyday problems in family relationships as we continue on our journey.

A KEY INVESTMENT PRINCIPLE

EVERY DAY DIFFERENT FORCES VIE FOR OUR ATTENTION—vocational, civic, or volunteer work. Each is important. Our task as men is to maintain the highest level of commitment to our greatest investment—our wives foremost, then our children. As we work to build strong marriages and families through love, protection, and biblical values, we can maintain our walk on this path to purity. Just as we constantly monitor our investments or check in with the stockbroker, we need constantly to monitor and improve our relationships with our wives and children. They are the greatest investments of our lives.

STRAIGHT TO THE PATH

When we are ill, most of us visit the doctor. It may take some coaxing but eventually we get there, take some medicine, and get over the illness. Sometimes that medicine sends us to bed for several days until it works through our system. When our families and marriages are in trouble, they need a strong prescription to begin to make a difference. Here are five areas to examine, with life-changing prescriptions from the Bible, to bring change to our homes and the people we love most.

1. Marriage Checkup. How are you investing in your wife—in her mind, soul, and body? Are you honoring your marriage? Hebrews 13:4 exhorts, "Marriage should be honored by all, and the marriage bed kept pure, for God will judge the adulterer and all the sexually immoral." What specific steps can you take to begin to honor and invest in your marriage? List several.

2. Time Checkup. How do we spend our time? Life passes in a whirlwind. It is easy for each of us to get caught up in our careers, church activities, civic duties, hobbies, or other interests that take time away from the family. Take several minutes to evaluate your priorities in relation to time with your family. Are you too busy to tuck your children into bed at night? Are you missing too many evening meals at home? Are you traveling too much? Are you so focused on your career that the family has slipped into second or third place in your life? What concrete actions can you take to put your priorities in better order and give your wife and children greater attention and time?

3. Father Checkup. Are you spending time encouraging and building up your children? Are you loyal to them and involved in their activities and sports? Are you teaching them to respect and obey you through exam-

ple and discipline? Fatherhood isn't a one-day experience, but a continuing journey of success or failure. We need to recommit ourselves to our children and our role as a father.

4. Spiritual Leadership Checkup. Are you modeling your spiritual values for your children and your wife? This doesn't have to be complicated or involved. It can mean praying together for a few minutes several times a week or reading the Bible as a family several times a week. We have a responsibility for spiritual leadership, according to 1 Timothy 3. Take a few minutes to evaluate that responsibility and how you are handling it. If you have fallen short of your expectations, make some decisions for improvement.

5. Management Checkup. How are you managing the family? Are you giving proper attention to the family finances and family activities? Many of us know how to manage our places of employment. We have learned through experience the right and wrong ways to manage people. Managing the family effectively may require some experimentation with techniques and principles. Use different techniques with the various children as necessary. Evaluate your role as a manager in the family and how you are guarding and protecting your children and wife. Is there any area that especially needs improvement? Make a plan and chart your progress.

Admittedly, this checkup will reveal some rough edges. That's okay. As you work through each of these checkups, you can expect to see a higher reading on your purity thermometer. Let's raise the mercury to new heights.

CHAPTER SIX

LOVE THE CHURCH

HARRY LIVED FOR THE WEEKENDS and the time it afforded for relaxation. Although Harry liked his job as a corporate executive in a Denver banking group, the weekends gave him a chance to kick off his shoes, watch some sports, and enjoy a few beers. He managed a few tasks around the house for his wife and kids, but he usually spent most of a weekend perched in front of the television set or, occasionally, taking his family to a movie.

On weekdays Harry had to get up at 5:00 A.M. to shower and shave for work. He arrived at his workplace at 7:00 A.M. and often stayed until late at night. Saturday and Sunday gave Harry that rare chance to sleep until noon and then relax. Why spoil it by spending time in church? Besides, he allowed his wife and children to attend a local church—wasn't that enough?

Harry had tried organized religion as a child. Every Sunday his parents packed him off to Sunday school. He acquired the idea then that church was boring and didn't have much relevance for his life. Harry even earned some attendance awards—but they abruptly became optional and insignificant the minute he turned eighteen and could decide for himself whether to attend church.

Harry would still attend church on the major holidays, such as Christmas and Easter. He also made it a point to attend whenever his children were involved in some special performance such as a Vacation Bible School program. Otherwise, he looked at church as a bother. Sleeping and relaxing were Harry's priorities for Sunday.

Many men let their wives attend church services with the children while they themselves avoid the House of Worship. Then there are others—like Jason McCauley—at the other end of the spectrum. They attend every week. If the church doors are open for any reason, Jason is present—but only in body. He attends the services to humor and please his wife, but his heart isn't in them. Mostly he uses the time for some mental gymnastics and planning his work for the next day.

My guess is that most of us can relate to Harry and Jason. Statistics show that the mainline churches continue to fall in membership. Maybe you're like Harry and have left the whole religion scene. You tried it as a small child—probably under duress—and crossed that off your list of possibilities. You decided that you didn't know the songs and didn't like the preaching or even the thought of putting on a coat and tie during the weekend. More likely, you have Jason's problem—you're there in body, but your mind is a thousand miles away.

I have good news for you. The church can be a critical part of your spiritual growth. It's a place where you can find other people who are also looking for spiritual answers to their everyday problems. It's a place where you can find people to support your concerns and needs through prayer and practical means as well. I guess you expect this kind of pep talk from a preacher, but I wouldn't be working for the church if I really thought it was a waste of time for men.

Here's a concept that is most important: The church isn't a place to come and just take from the service. It's a place where you can give back—not just money, but in other ways. We need each other, and church is an excellent place to find kindred spirits and grow in your commitment to God's Word.

Like any new relationship, "church" doesn't start out with a deep love. It begins with a friendship or examination phase, then moves into a deeper friendship; finally, you will discover a love relationship with the church. We are not talking about organized religion or a building; we have in mind here what the apostle Paul talks about as "the body of Christ." The church in America is made up of many parts. We can't take our hand or our big toe and say, "We don't need you. We'll cut you off from our body." Rather, each part is necessary in order to have a complete body. That is the way it is with the church. Obviously, no church is perfect. But that doesn't mean that we can afford to ignore it completely. We need this spiritual connection along our path to purity.

FIND A SPIRITUAL CONNECTION

IF YOU DON'T HAVE A CHURCH, how do you find a good one? If you look under *Church* in the phone book, you will encounter numerous choices—probably right in your neighborhood. The American church has been fractured and splintered throughout history. If a group of people didn't like a particular teaching, they started a new church. Instead of trying to work together, they split off into a new branch, and eventually that branch became a denomination.

Here are several guidelines for finding a church:

The Denomination Doesn't Matter. You may be surprised to see this statement here, because I am a bishop in a particular denomination. I am expected to display a denominational label. But if you ask such a question with a predetermined answer, maybe you are building a denominational wall in your life.

Consider your relationships with friends, acquaintances, neighbors, and co-workers. Do you relate well only to those who attend your church? It's fairly easy to hide behind the label of "Pentecostal" or "Charismatic" or "Baptist" or "Catholic" or "Episcopal" or even "Nondenominational."

In years past, it *was* important which denomination I aligned myself with. I am a third-generation member of the Church of God in Christ, and early in life I was exposed to many religious persuasions. Around Enid and other small Oklahoma towns, I spoke in various churches and community meetings, as I related in chapter 1. As a nineteen-year-old boy in the summer of 1956, I felt called to become a full-time pastor. Immediately after this decision, I traveled to my uncle's farm in northeastern Oklahoma. When I arrived, I told my uncle about my plans to go into the ministry. My uncle served as a lay youth minister on the staff of the First Baptist Church of Nowata, Oklahoma. He responded, "Great! I'm glad the Lord called you to the gospel ministry, Phil. I want you to bring the message to our youth meeting this summer."

In a parochial way, I protested, saying, "I can't do that." To my way of thinking, I was completely committed to the Pentecostal ways of the Church of God in Christ. How could I preach my first sermon in a Baptist church? It would tarnish my reputation forever! But my uncle was persistent and scheduled my message for about a month later. Every day I agonized over this opportunity. Many times my uncle asked me, "How are you coming, Phil, on preparing your message?"

Each time I responded, "I can't do it, Uncle."

Then my uncle said, "You can't say that, Phil. You've *got* to do it." Out of respect for my uncle, I began to prepare my sermon—erratically. The day before I was scheduled to speak, I rode in from the fields on my uncle's tractor. My uncle said, "Well, Son, how are you doing? You know tomorrow is your big day."

I said, "I told you I can *not* do that."

He said, "Oh, yeah, you've got to speak! We've got the word out, and everybody is expecting you to preach. As a matter of fact, you take the rest of the day off, go up to your room, and get yourself together. You'll find some helpful books in that room."

I gave up my protest and went inside. I felt distraught and emotionally torn about preaching a sermon in the Baptist church. My denominational roots went deep. How could I turn my back on my Pentecostal background and give my first message in a Baptist church? I went to my room, which was located in the attic of the house. I flipped through a couple of my uncle's books, but I still couldn't find anything worthwhile to say at the service.

As I read, I prayed, "Dear God, maybe I missed You. Maybe You didn't call me into the ministry. Lord, it seems strange that a Holiness boy preaches his first official message to a Baptist congregation. Something is wrong with this picture!" I argued with God about the wrongness of this scheduled meeting, yet I didn't fully understand the mysterious ways of God.

In a burst of creativity, I devised a solution to my problem. I prayed, "God, I'll even get up there tomorrow morning and tell them that I made a mistake. I wasn't called to preach there. God, please don't let me preach a sermon."

As I continued to pray, I fell into a dreamlike state in which the Lord gave me a panoramic view of my future. In this dream I climbed a long set of stairs that wound up outside a building that had the appearance of a state capital building. I climbed each step slowly, one at a time, and did whatever was required. After I finished my task on a particular step, a great applause rang throughout the hall. Then I climbed another step and performed before another audience. When I finished speaking, the crowd gave another round of loud applause.

Each step represented an area of my life and a significant action for other people. In my dream I climbed all the way through my life until I reached the very top platform—the highest mark for my life. There, as with the other steps, I did what God required me to do. My performance was impeccable, and at the conclusion I knew it was perfect. Unlike the other times, when I finished this message, the crowd was strangely silent and gave no applause.

Finally, I finished my performance and bowed to the audience. As I bowed, the curtain began to close in front of me. As it did so, I remained in the bowed position for a long time. I was waiting for some response from the audience and could not comprehend why no one applauded.

I was stunned. Tears filled my eyes and my heart. I had given my best performance of all to this final audience—yet there came no response. I stood behind the closed curtain for what seemed like an eternity, although it was actually only about five minutes. I started to stand erect. As I did so, I could hear a great applause break through from the other side of the curtain. People clapped. They whistled. They yelled, "Come back! Encore! Return!" My heavy feelings of sadness lifted, and it was marvelous to hear such a response. With great excitement, I tried to find the slit in the curtain and return to the crowd for my encore. Frantically, I searched through one seam of the curtain to the other, but could not locate an opening. My performance was indeed finished. There would be no encore.

As I thought about the meaning of this dream, the Lord seemed to be saying that my life would be one in which I was called to do what was required, to serve the people—at any level—until I reached the top. The real applause and importance of my life wouldn't come until the end.

I received a great deal of comfort from this dream because I knew that no matter what happened in my life, my course would be directed by the Lord of the Universe. Also, through this dream, I felt that I should move ahead and preach my first sermon in the Baptist church. This action set a course for my life that has continually crossed denominational lines. The next year I received my first summer job—as a camp counselor for the Disciples of Christ. In 1963, I was living in Denver while preparing for my ordination. The state meeting for the Church of God in Christ was being held in a Christian Methodist Episcopal church, so that was the site of my ordination service.

These three key events set a pattern for my life. For many years, the focus of my work was on my denominational affiliation and that focus became so strong that I excluded the whole body of Christ. But eventually, instead of staying in a single denomination, the Church of God in Christ, God has permitted me to be involved in a wide range of denominations and churches and has enlarged my vision of the church of Jesus Christ. This has broken down an important barrier in my own life as well as helped me to lower denominational walls between Christians.

Please don't misunderstand me. A denomination isn't bad, but we cannot allow the denomination to become exclusive to the total body of Christ. Racism was perpetuated by my denominational affiliation. The Church of God in Christ is predominantly African American. From an early age, I had been taught an exclusive attitude: "As a black person, I may be struggling with my current circumstances, but for the long haul, I am headed to heaven and spending eternity with the Lord Jesus. And those white devils who mistreat us in the name of Jesus as well as those 'sectarian' folks? We know they are going to face an eternity in hell." During the 1930s and 1940s, this sort of divisive attitude allowed us to hang on and get through those difficult days and nights of segregation. Every place had signs that said, "White Only" or "No Coloreds Allowed." We sat in the back of buses and had access only through the rear doors of restaurants. At the movie houses, we sat in "our place"— the balcony. Accordingly, we figured that white people were going to hell. Where else would they spend eternity when they treated us in this manner?

Because of my personal relationship with Christ, I reached beyond the persecution and separation of my past. During my lifetime I have met and become friends with many wonderful white people from a wide variety of church backgrounds.

When I am asked, "Where do you go to church?" my first response is, "I'm a Christian and love the Lord Jesus." So when you look for a church, don't let the denomination get in the way. As we walk the path of purity, our bond is Christ and not a denomination.

Size Isn't Important. Churches come in all sizes, from megachurches with multiple services to small churches with only a few people attending. There are various styles of worship services. Some services are very structured and the congregation follows the service on a program; others are more spontaneous. In some churches, the priest or pastor wears a robe and a clerical collar. In others, the minister wears a suit; and in still others, the pastor is dressed in a sweater with no tie.

My own bent toward the small church was nurtured from my earliest memories of my dad. One of his great passions was to serve as a pastor to small congregations around our hometown of Perry, Oklahoma. I tagged along with him when he led services in these churches. I remember going with him to a little Indian reservation outside Perry.

When I was about a year and a half, our family moved to Enid, Oklahoma. The Church of God in Christ assigned Dad to a log-cabin church in Crescent, which was about fifty miles southeast of Perry. To Dad, being assigned to this church signified his arrival as a pastor—even though he had been preaching for many years.

Because this congregation was too small to hire Dad full-time, he maintained a janitorial service in Enid. Two or three times a week, Dad would drive to the church. The first thing he would do in the winter was unlock the door and light a fire in the woodstove. In the summer he would open the windows first. Next, Dad would pick up the members who mostly lived within a five-block radius of the church. These were all older women with some children or grandchildren, so Dad made sure each of them got to church.

The church service began with prayer and singing. Then they passed the offering plate. The collection usually amounted to $1.50 or $3.00—never more than $5.00. After preaching his message, Dad turned out the lights, then did everything in reverse and took his members home.

Often during our drive back to Enid that night, Dad would run out of gas. He would walk to the next town for gas, or sometimes we would both wait in the car until the early morning hours. We were praying that someone would stop and get us some gasoline.

My dad's commitment to the church, and his life of faith reflected in that ministry, have been a large role model for my own life and ministry.

As you select a church, consider these matters:

- Do I want to form some relationships with these people that can endure week after week?
- Is the church friendly and welcoming?
- Is the program of the church meeting my needs? (For example, if you have children, you want to discuss your choices with the children. Some churches have a more extensive youth ministry than others. Some youth ministers are better suited than others to working with teenagers. Your children and their spiritual needs may influence your place of worship.)

Evaluate the Church with Some Key Criteria. When you attend any church, there are a few critical points to evaluate. First, is Christ preached there? This should be our foremost concern regarding any church. Does the church love Jesus Christ?

Examine the beliefs of the church. Ask the pastor or a key leader in the church about its beliefs. Many churches have a "doctrinal statement" or creed that expresses what it teaches.

What does the church believe about God—does He exist in three persons: the Father, the Son, and the Holy Spirit? Commonly called the Trinity, this doctrine is an important benchmark for a local church.

What does the church believe about the Bible? Are the Scriptures an active part of the church service or the daily life of the congregation? Some churches selectively look at the Bible and don't believe parts of it. You want to find a church that believes that the entire Bible is God's written revelation to mankind and is verbally inspired, authoritative, and without error in the original manuscripts. This belief about the Bible is important, because without this as a base, the church leaders can pick and choose from the Bible rather than taking it as the whole truth of God.

What does the church, as believers in Jesus Christ, believe about the Holy Spirit? The Holy Spirit performs the miracle of the new birth in an unbeliever and lives inside believers. Through the power of the Spirit in our lives, we are able to live godly lives. Make sure you check the church's perspective about the Holy Spirit.

As we search for a church, we can learn from the life of Zacchaeus (see Luke 19:1–10). Zacchaeus was a tax collector, and a successful one at that. He had clawed his way to the top of the professional ladder, but he wasn't happy. It wasn't just that his trade made him very unpopular. It was that he had a hunger in his heart and soul that worldly success couldn't fill. In many ways, the dilemma of Zacchaeus is mirrored in our daily life and work.

Then Zacchaeus learned that Jesus was coming to town. *Jesus is a lowly Nazarene. He doesn't have any social standing,*

Zacchaeus thought. *Yet He commands the attention of people from all walks of life. Even the children follow Jesus. Why?*

Zacchaeus soon met the Master, and all his questions were answered. He was overwhelmed with the magnitude and power of Jesus Christ. And he was immediately transformed. He told Jesus, "Look, Lord! Here and now I give half of my possessions to the poor; and if I have cheated anybody out of anything, I will pay back four times the amount" (v. 8).

Jesus recognized that Zacchaeus was a changed man and told him, "Today salvation has come to this house. . . . For the Son of Man came to seek and to save what was lost" (vv. 9–10).

When Jesus is in our life, we change. When He is in our soul, He gives us the means for total change. He gives us a compassion for the poor and turns our greed into giving. I call this the "Zacchean Principle" of the changing power of Jesus Christ. Our changing is based on the fact that we have a personal relationship with the Savior.

Seek out a church where Jesus is preached and loved.

Perfect Churches Need Not Apply. The final principle for selecting a church is that you not look for the perfect one. You will never find it. Every church has flaws. Some churches will seem too large for you. Some won't seem friendly and warm enough. Some may have a limited youth program. Others have a small choir or a young pastor. Perhaps the church has a parking problem.

Some people waste years church-hopping without ever settling on one as a church home. One Sunday they feel like going to a Pentecostal service, and the next week they love the tradition of an Episcopal church. A third Sunday they go to another part of town to listen to a particular pastor. Because they fail to commit their family to a particular church, they remain unknown to the church community. They don't know either the pastor or the people in the next row. Avoid this kind of situation, because it is not conducive to your spiritual growth.

In our search for God, we may be attracted by the fast foods of our culture. By "fast foods" I mean the appeal of getting something quickly with little effort or personal investment. The number one infomercial for revenue earnings during 1995 was the Psychic Friends Network. People are searching for spirituality and for $4.99 a minute, they can call a 900 number and get in touch with a spiritual psychic. It's fast—but it's not a true relationship with the God of the Universe. True spirituality finds its source of strength in the Bible, the written Word of God—not in some extra book or reference tool, but simply in the words of Scripture.

We can encounter "fast food" in church as well, in the form of a dazzling choir or an eloquent preacher. Don't be taken in by a strong personality or a slick public relations campaign. It is wise to return to my single best rule for finding a spiritual connection: Is Christ preached, and is He preached from the Scriptures? If you use this yardstick, it will be difficult for you to go wrong.

AFTER YOU HAVE FOUND A CHURCH, THEN WHAT?

THERE ARE MANY EXCELLENT CHURCHES across the United States—in large and small cities. God has given each of us the freedom to select the place that best suits our needs and particular situation. I have given you some general criteria to use in your search. So now suppose you have found a church in which you can grow spiritually through preaching, worshiping God, and enjoying fellowship with other

Christians. What do you do next? I believe you should also be in a church where you can give something back to it. If you look for a place to serve within the church, I'm sure you can find your niche.

For some, the first thing that comes to mind is teaching. Yes, the church needs good teachers in the Sunday school classes, and perhaps you have this ability. By contrast, you may be a man whose knees begin to shake and quiver if you are asked to teach. Perhaps your work schedule doesn't allow you the preparation time that teaching would require. There is no need to worry, because there are many other opportunities for service within a church besides teaching.

First, consider your skills and talents. Make a short list of your work-related and hobby-related skills. Use them in the church. Here are some starter ideas to trigger your thinking—the list could be endless:

- Drive the church van or bus.
- Make visits to nursing homes, hospitals, or jails.
- Purchase office supplies for the church.
- Paint some rooms, or make repairs.
- Help with the janitorial duties.
- Assist the pastor with calling on visitors.
- Set up chairs for functions, or help prepare the church for Sunday services.
- Shovel the sidewalks during the winter.

Whether the task is large or small, you can be active in serving your church. Let me add one note of caution, however. Some pastors are quick to overextend an eager volunteer. It can be abusive and possibly detrimental to your family and other aspects of your life if you serve to an excessive extent. Use wisdom in your service for the local church, and don't be afraid to tell the pastor that you're overloaded or can't take on a particular task. The key principle is balance.

UNDERSTAND THE PASTOR

MOST PEOPLE DON'T REALIZE IT, but being the pastor is one of the loneliest positions in a church. Many people feel that their pastor should be at their beck and call twenty-four hours a day. No matter what the need or what the crisis, they call their pastor for strength and counsel. Pastors have immense demands placed upon them. They need to prepare a sermon—sometimes several—every week. It takes time to study the Scriptures and prepare a solid message that will minister to the people.

Pastors are also expected to fulfill traditional services for the congregation such as weddings and funerals and visiting the sick and encouraging people in times of crisis. Over the years, I have often been called on to go to the local courthouse and testify for members of my congregation or sit in the courtroom with family members of someone on trial. There are many and various demands on the life of a pastor. I don't begrudge these, but I want you to understand that another key part of your path to purity is to serve your pastor by exercising wisdom and discretion in what you require of him.

During my first ten years as the pastor of All Nations Church of God in Christ, the women outnumbered the men—about seventeen to one. Women became central from the beginning of my pastorate.

I know the challenge of a church that lacks men. We needed men to drive the church bus, to shovel snow in the winter and care for the lawn in the summer, and to assist

me in visiting the elderly and sick. But at the outset, the
women of the church did everything. They taught Sunday
school and served as the pastor's assistants. In late 1973, a
number of men began to attend the church. One of these,
Ralph Petaway, was retired from the U.S. Army and had
relocated to the Denver area. He became a deacon in the
church and eventually my administrative assistant. With his
diligence and service, Ralph provided great leadership to
our church. He was the first of several men who have joined
the ranks of leadership. Every church needs men. You can
serve a vital and important part in the life of the church
through your involvement.

Across America, pastors are gaining more and more support from the men in their churches. One of the key principles of Promise Keepers is a commitment to help the local
pastor in a fresh and different way. Too often, there is no
mutual care for the local pastor, yet we need to honor and
respect the shepherds. Hebrews 13:17 says, "Obey your
leaders and submit to their authority. They keep watch over
you as men who must give an account. Obey them so that
their work will be a joy, not a burden, for that would be of
no advantage to you." The pastor is accountable for the care
of the souls of his congregation, but he shouldn't have to
carry this great responsibility alone.

The apostle Paul repeats this principle in 1 Corinthians
9:14: "The Lord has commanded that those who preach the
gospel should receive their living from the gospel." A church
or congregation needs to see that a pastor receives essentials
such as a livable wage, care for his family, adequate health
insurance, clothing and transportation, funds for retirement,
and times for rest and personal study and vacation. Too often
churches don't provide these necessities to their pastors.

Consequently, pastors become worn out emotionally, physically, and spiritually. Many men have fallen prey to difficulties because no one came alongside to help them.

Promise Keepers has stirred a commitment in the hearts of men to connect with their pastors in many practical ways. In my more than thirty years as a pastor, I have come to know well the need for men of strong commitment and service to stand by me.

OTHER WAYS TO SERVE YOUR PASTOR

BESIDES YOUR ACTIVE INVOLVEMENT in the life and service of the church, you can help your pastor several other ways.

Pray for Your Pastor. James 5:16 tells us that "the prayer of a righteous man is powerful and effective." Here are some specifics to pray regarding the spiritual leader of your church:

- Ask God to protect this leader from failure and sin. We all fail daily, and only as we have God's strength and power in our lives will we be able to withstand temptation.
- Ask God to give your pastor wisdom for the multitude of decisions—large and small—that he faces every day.
- Ask God to give your pastor sincere friendships. Your pastor needs people around him with whom he can let down his guard or take off his face mask. These people will guard his confidences and not gossip, but simply pray for their leader. Each pastor needs these Christlike friendships to stave off feelings of loneliness.
- Pray for your pastor's family. Historically, many church leaders have been overabsorbed in their work for God

to the detriment of their families. Ask the Lord to give special times and relationships to each member of the pastor's family. Be specific in your prayers; pray for the pastor's wife and children by name.

- Ask God to help your pastor continually grow in his faith and his personal relationship with Jesus Christ. Pastors are busy people and sometimes neglect to spend the necessary time in study of the Scriptures, prayer, and fasting. Pray that your pastor will continually grow more and more like Jesus.

- Depending on the size of your church, pray for every member of the church staff—the associate pastors, the assistants, the Sunday school teachers, and the church secretaries. Ask for God to bless and honor the lives of each of these servants.

- Consider being a part of a team of intercessors who continually pray for the pastor, the church, and its outreaches. In my church I have organized a team of seventy-five people who have agreed to pray for me continually.

- Finally, make a point to tell your pastor that you are praying for him. Let him know that you will be praying for him on a continuing basis and that he can approach you with specific prayer requests held in confidence.

EVERY LOVE RELATIONSHIP TAKES WORK

IT DOESN'T MATTER THE RELATIONSHIP—a marriage, a church, or the workplace. Every love relationship requires a commitment to ensure that it will remain and will keep on growing. Love is not something that is done once and for all. It is not without difficulties and setbacks. But your commitment to the church is a critical relationship. As men, we need to love the church and foster our relationship with it. Church offers us an opportunity to give as well as receive. Through your charity toward your pastor, you will receive God's blessing on your life and the assurance of spiritual answers to the problems of your everyday life.

STRAIGHT TO THE PATH

1. Get behind the pulpit. That is, support your pastor in every possible way. Maybe you are asking why you should be the one to help your pastor. The Bible makes clear the importance God places on pastors; the Creator of the Universe has called them to be the caretakers of His people. Jeremiah 3:15 (KJV) says, "I will give you pastors according to mine heart, which shall feed you with knowledge and understanding."

2. Support the pastor with your time. After you have found a church home, a critical step on your path to purity is to support your pastor. That support may take the form of a friendship or an essential service. Consider your gifts and talents. Are you good at construction or building? There may be maintenance projects that you could fit into your schedule. Do you operate a business or manage funds or people? How can you use that experience in the House of God and assist the pastor or his staff? If God has blessed you financially, then pass that blessing along to your church.

    Pastors often feel alone in carrying the burdens and responsibilities of the church. Yet the Bible reminds us that the pastor is the teacher and leader of the church—not the whole church all by himself. How can you show friendship? Invite your pastor to lunch and talk about how you can help him. Don't assume that you know his needs without asking. Then when you find out those needs, make a consistent effort to help and support your pastor.

3. Reach out to the support staff. Many churches have assistant pastors, business managers, or others on staff. How can you help these people in a practical way? Take the time to encourage them, whether by a note or a phone call or a commitment to pray for them daily. Be creative in your ideas and means of encouragement.

4. What is your skill? Use it for God. Offer it to the church. Be specific about the amount of time you can commit and what you can do. Your service might be a single occasion or something that extends over six months or a year. God has given each of us a talent. Plan how to use your talent for Him.

5. Support the church financially. The church can operate only from the gifts of God's people. Paul writes in 2 Corinthians 9:6–7, "Remember this: Whoever sows sparingly will also reap sparingly, and whoever sows generously will also reap generously. Each man should give what he has decided in his heart to give, not reluctantly or under compulsion, for God loves a cheerful giver." I have seen this principle operate in my own life. As I joyfully give to the church, God returns the blessing to me. You can also experience such blessing as you support the church with your finances.

6. Honor the pastor for his service and acts of ministry. Serving the church can be a thankless task. How can you honor your pastor? How many years or months has he served your congregation? Can you organize a celebration when he reaches a certain milestone? Don't

let his actions pass without proper recognition from the church.

7. Commit yourself to pray for your pastor. We expect our shepherd, or pastor, to be praying for us. In the same way, we can minister to him through prayer. Pray for his work. Pray for his spiritual life—like us, pastors can experience times of spiritual drought. Pray for his family. Pray for protection for him. Ask God to use your pastor's leadership in a powerful way to draw others to Jesus Christ.

You can pray for your pastor anytime and anywhere. You can take a few minutes during your break at work or while driving in your car. It is important that we pray for our leaders along our path to purity.

CHAPTER SEVEN

WHEN WILL PEOPLE WORK TOGETHER?

IF YOU HAVEN'T NOTICED YET, I am an African American—a black man serving a largely white organization. I have grown up in black churches, but I have spoken in a lot of white churches. In many ways, my life answers the question, "Can black and white Christians get along?" We can. And we should. But often, we don't. From my stories of reconciliation and my personal experience, I would like to tell you what I think about racial reconciliation.

True reconciliation will not happen from laws or enforcement of the laws—although we need both. It will not come from protests or marches—even though these had their place in our nation's history. True unity comes from building relationships across racial and denominational barriers. We have erected emotional and spiritual walls so that we aren't involved with people who are different from us. These walls must be torn down if we are to discover the sixth path to purity—a movement of reconciliation.

Recently I organized a meeting with more than a hundred African American leaders from the church, politics, and business. We called this meeting "The Chairman's Report, An Appointment with Destiny." Leaders from different denominations discussed how to foster greater cooperation. We fully recognized that there are difficulties of blacks working together with blacks, much less reaching across the racial barriers to work with people of other races.

The founder and CEO of Promise Keepers, Coach Bill McCartney, said that the church should be the first place to eradicate racism. He believes that through the work of reconciliation we can accomplish this goal during our lifetime. While Coach Mac's words ring true about the eradication of racism beginning in the church, I know it will only happen through men becoming completely surrendered to Jesus Christ. Nothing else will work.

My childhood home was right on the line between the black and white communities in Enid, Oklahoma. As a small boy, I played house with the white girl across the street. She was the momma, and I was the daddy. We always played on our property and never at her house. Segregation was the rule of the day, and I never questioned where we played. I just understood that black people and white people lived completely separate lives.

One reason that I have had a long-term interest in reconciliation is the example of my dad. One time as a teenager, I accompanied my father to an IGA grocery store located some distance from the "Negro" district. My dad bent down for an item on the bottom shelf when suddenly a white man came up behind him and kicked him—a solid boot in the backside! My dad was a good-sized man of around 250 pounds, and I was already a well-developed and successful boxer.

When Dad was kicked, I was shocked—but waited to see how my father would respond. Slowly he straightened up, then deliberately faced his assailant. The man blurted out that he had wanted to "kick his butt" for a long time. I could feel the anger swelling in my chest. I was ready to square off with this guy. I just knew my dad and I could put a hurt on this man.

But my dad, a "tent-making" pastor, faced the man squarely with strength and poise, then said, "As long as you're a white guy and I'm a black man, don't you ever raise your foot and kick me again." Then my dad said, "Come on, son. We're getting out of here." To turn and walk out without a fight didn't seem like a proper response to me, and I was full of pain as I followed my dad out of the store. I wanted to wear that guy out! As we rode down the street, I asked, "Dad, why? He had no right to treat you like that!"

"I know he had no right, Son," Dad said. He explained that men like that didn't see us as people but were ignorant and afraid.

Dad taught me the value of forgiveness in the midst of our pain. From this experience and others, I learned that I had a clear choice for action. I could be angry and bitter, or I could forgive others because they didn't know what they were doing. Then I could leave that hurt with God and trust that the Maker of the Universe would leave us free in our spirit.

Along our path to purity, we will encounter people who are full of prejudice and set against any type of reconciliation. These people will often revile us and give us additional pain. Like my dad, we will receive some unexpected "kicks." My natural response is to double my fist and look for a means of revenge. As a believer in Christ and a person who has God's Spirit inside me, I have to turn and offer for-giveness instead. Then the bitterness won't grow inside and I can be free in God's Spirit to receive His creative ideas for corrective action.

HOW TO HANDLE REJECTION

REJECTION HAPPENS TO EVERYONE, whether on a large or small scale. When we are young, we reach out and try to date the opposite sex. We get turned down and feel rejected. Or we apply to a specific university or college and don't get accepted for admission. Or possibly we apply to a corpora-tion and don't get the job because someone else was selected.

In chapter 3, I told briefly about my outright rejection from a social service job because of skin color. From this experience and others, I have learned three important prin-ciples that will help you when you face rejection along the path to reconciliation. These principles can apply whether the rejection is the result of race or denomination or any other sort of barrier between people.

1. *When a door of opportunity closes, don't turn bitter.* The Bible warns us against bitterness in Hebrews 12:15: "See to it that no one misses the grace of God and that no bitter root grows up to cause trouble and defile many." If it is allowed to fester, bitterness will root itself and cause trou-ble not only for you but for many others. Turn to God and forgive the person who wronged you rather than hold onto the bitterness.

2. *Lean on your faith in God and look for another oppor-tunity.* When one door slams shut, expect God to open another somewhere. A key lesson for the life of faith is to

trust in God's direction for every day. Lamentations 3:22–23 reminds of this important lesson:

> Because of the LORD's great love we are not consumed,
>   for his compassions never fail.
> They are new every morning;
>   great is your faithfulness.

If you have made a personal commitment to Jesus Christ, then God faithfully directs and guides your life. You can move ahead with the expectation that God will make another way. As the popular song from Don Moen says,

> God will make a way,
> where there seems to be no way.
> He moves in ways we cannot see.
> God will make a way for me.

Whenever you face such a situation, it's an opportunity to lean on the capable hands of God.

3. Don't beat your head against a brick wall. Work with people who are willing to work with you. Everyone wants to be liked and respected by the people who cross their paths in life. Unfortunately, this desire to be liked can interfere with our progress. While I want to work hard at my relationships and be reconciled with my fellowmen, at the same time I don't want to continually try to break down a brick wall. Let us assume that you have prayed and asked God to guide your life and relationships. He wants you to work with those people who will work with you. Let the other relationships go—release them from your tightly clenched hand.

Sometimes if we are willing to let go, that person will have second thoughts and restore the relationship. At other

times, the person will disappear from our lives and we will
move into a new series of relationships. The point is that
we move ahead and don't continually try to fix something
that isn't ready or can't be fixed. Use this principle in handling the rejection of reconciliation: Work with those
people who will work with you, and let the rest go.

THE COST OF RECONCILIATION

ONE DAY, QUITE INNOCENTLY, I said something sharp to a
member of my church whom I will call John. I didn't know
my words came across as "sharp," but they hurt John. Over
the next few days, John took time to think about the pain I
had caused. Taking a deep breath, he asked for an appointment to meet with me, but gave me no clue as to what was
on his mind.

When he entered the room, I could tell John had a
weighty matter to discuss. Was it his family? Or his work?
No. To my surprise, it was me.

John said, "Pastor, the other day your words came
across to me as sharp and stinging. It hurt me when you
said _____."

I listened to John and replied, "Well, I had no idea that
my words would affect you like that. In fact, I don't even
remember saying those words." I didn't immediately ask for
his forgiveness, but thought about the pain that John had
expressed. In fact, I had buried my own hurt and pain about
the incident. In the pressure of the moment, I had gone on
to some other activity.

Now, with this confrontation from John, my pain resur-
faced. My old wound began to sting and bleed again. John
watched as I silently processed his words, and then he said
with disgust, "Well, just forget it! You can't forgive me, and

there is no sense of forgiveness from you. We can't be reconciled." Bewildered, I watched John stomp out of the room.

What was that all about? Did John want to be reconciled to me? He acted like it, but when it came right down to it, no, John didn't want to go through any process of reconciliation.

From John's perspective, he felt that he had attempted reconciliation. But in reality, he took the initial step of confrontation and then quit. Real reconciliation takes time, energy, and patience.

Often our world tries to put Band-Aids on racial prejudice instead of honestly facing the pain of the past. Are we willing to look beyond the surface at our differences and understand each other? It costs.

Many white people wonder why they have to deal with the pain their forefathers caused black people. "Why do we have to face the pain of our past?" they ask. "Can't we deal with the here and now without facing the past?" The answer is no. All of us are products of our past. True, you didn't own slaves, but my people were enslaved by your people. We can't just sweep that under the rug. Why not?

Present-day white Americans must realize the repercussions of past actions. Because of their race, white Americans have become the leaders of the world; they are the most educated and have the most power in our society. How did this happen and at what price?

America was built on hard work, commitment, and accomplishment. When the English settlers arrived in the country, they met the Native Americans. These Native Americans were willing to share their secrets for living in this country and raising their crops. If some of these Native Americans were unwilling to help, then their lives were forfeited. Essentially, the Native American became a stepping-stone for the white American. The whites moved ahead and conquered the United States at the expense of the Native Americans.

Into the foundation stone of the white Americans was etched a commitment to put God first in their lives and to seek a place of worship. But to the Native Americans, it meant giving their life's blood. If they didn't cooperate and give up their land, they were killed. Our white forefathers decided to work the land, but they needed indentured servants from overseas. They went abroad to Africa and brought slaves to America.

A significant part of slavery was that the Africans had to give up their identity, their names, their culture, and their sense of self-worth. Every attribute they gave up in slavery contributed to their dehumanization. These Africans were strong and spiritually directed people. For them to give up their humanity was no transitory, simple experience.

The African male was a natural-born storyteller. The pride of his life was to tell stories and pass along history to younger generations. But as a slave, he suppressed this storytelling ability as well as forfeited his music, culture, and creativity. His family was torn apart, its members separated and sold. In the new world of the United States, this grown man became a laborer, or "boy," who could never become a man. The dehumanization process took years and many stages to bring down the African American man to such a low level.

The understanding of this dehumanization process helps us—black and white—to identify the pain and effort of reconciliation. We must begin to understand the journey of another person and his ancestors to be reconciled to each other as brothers and sisters in Christ.

The African American, the Hispanic, and the Native American had each become less than a human being. None of these groups were considered equals with the whites in terms of the opportunity to worship, their housing, their living conditions, their education, or even their food. They were not properly compensated for their work.

With this background and history of the races in mind, you can begin to glimpse the difficulty of racial reconciliation. A white person comes to me and wants to be reconciled. He says, "I've worked through the past and the pain. Jesus Christ is in my life. Let's be brothers."

I ask the person, "Can you feel the pain of my past? Do you really understand how we are different?" Until this person comes face-to-face with the reality of my past, it is difficult for us to be reconciled.

MY JOURNEY ON THE PATH OF RECONCILIATION

THE STEPS TO PURITY ARE NOT A ONETIME AFFAIR but an often repeated process. In my life, I tried to find this purification process through integration. "Tried" is the operative word. I spent my early years in the black community of Enid, attended an all-black high school, and planned to attend an all-black institution, Lincoln University in Jefferson City, Missouri. But the Supreme Court decision of 1954 changed my world. In the case of *Brown vs. Board of Education of Topeka,* the U.S. Supreme Court declared that the "separate but equal doctrine" that had prevailed since the nineteenth century was wrong. Schools were thereafter required to integrate. I wanted to do my part to make it happen.

Phillips University in Enid intended to become integrated. I grew up in a Pentecostal Holiness church, and my heritage was steeped in the Church of God in Christ. Phillips was a liberal arts university affiliated with the Disciples of Christ denomination.

In spring 1955, Phillips University consulted my local high school to see whether any black students qualified to enroll. The high school principal, Luther W. Elliott Sr., said, "I know just the guy for you—Phillip Porter." Through my public speaking and Golden Glove boxing, combined with my academic excellence, I was well-known in the school and the community. To me, Phillips seemed like a good choice because it was a "Christian" university. Little did I know how much the university would be a part of my path to purity.

One afternoon, Professor Elliott took me to meet the university president, Dr. Eugene S. Briggs. We sat in the high-back, deep-red leather chairs of his office. Through the local newspaper, Dr. Briggs had followed my success in boxing and knew my academic qualifications.

"There's one thing more, Phillip," Dr. Briggs said as the meeting was drawing to an end. "Integration will not be without problems. We've never had black students living in close proximity to white students. This is a Christian college, and we're trying to integrate peacefully. We know about your successful fights in boxing, and I want your promise that you will not fight." I assured Dr. Briggs that my fighting days were over.

"You'll have to take a lot of flak from people, Phillip," Dr. Briggs continued. "Can you do it?"

"I'll be calm in any situation," I promised the president.

Our first day of student orientation was held on the baseball field. On this hot August afternoon, long tables were set up with watermelon. I walked through the crowd and carried my piece of melon. I would smile at people and make light conversation. As the only black male, I wanted to fit into my new school. But just when I didn't expect it, a big red-headed boy from Louisiana rushed out and pushed my face into my watermelon. As the juice ran down my face and shirt, he laughed, saying, "I always wanted to put a nigger's face in a melon."

In the heat of this moment, I forgot my promise to Dr. Briggs. With some rage, I put my boxing skills to use on this white boy and whipped him. Within minutes, both of us were in Dr. Briggs's office.

The President shook his head, expressing his disappointment. "Phillip, I told you integration would be difficult. You promised me that you wouldn't fight, and before classes even start, you are fighting." I apologized for getting embroiled in the fight.

Because the other student began the fight, he was immediately suspended and sent back home to Louisiana. After he left the room, Dr. Briggs turned to me.

"You need to keep yourself under control, Phillip," he cautioned. "You may face things worse than this during your years at Phillips University."

For the rest of my college years, I wasn't drawn into another fight. While there were plenty of opportunities, I resisted the temptation to lash back with my fists.

I was committed to the principle of integration and the process of integration. I even pledged an all-white Social Services Club. During pledge week we were blindfolded, and the members fed me what they called "frog eggs." They stuck their fingers down my throat and made sure I swallowed whatever it was they fed me. Eventually I got sick to my stomach from the ordeal. To this day, I have no idea what they fed me. I didn't care, because I was involved in the noble process of integration—whatever it took. I believed the path of my life was integration. It was only later that I realized that I needed to be on the path of following Jesus Christ alone.

From my intense desire for integration, sometimes I blended into my environment too much. While I was on the speech squad at Phillips, we traveled to different universities for our competitions. Often during these trips, as the only black member of the team, I slept and ate in a separate location from the others. But on one of our trips to Kansas, I was housed with the white students. In my subconscious, I forgot who I was and where I was. In a sense, I became white.

As I was eating breakfast, I looked up at a nearby mirror and saw a black hand. I suddenly moved my hand and thought, *Whose black hand is that?* It was a daunting moment—a pivotal moment—when I realized that the black hand was mine. Sometimes I tended to be ashamed of my blackness, and as a full-fledged member of this team, I felt I had made it in the white man's world—but I had carried my experience too far.

My revelation left me feeling broken and hurt. As a student of sociology, I had learned an important lesson about the process of integration and the steps to honoring Jesus Christ. That morning in Kansas, I got up from the table and didn't eat my breakfast. I realized I had blended in so well that I had given up my identity. I thought, *We're all white folks here together on this speech squad.* But I wasn't white. I know now that part of our search for identity entails being solid in our identity in Christ. This identity with Christ isn't something external, like something coming through the pores of our skin. The transformation is internal. The path to purity transcends racism and all other barriers. Our first obligation is to honor Jesus Christ and follow the standard of the Bible.

BURNING CHURCHES—SYMPTOMS OF THE WALLS THAT DIVIDE US

ACROSS AMERICA, A NUMBER OF CHURCH BURNINGS in the southern United States during 1995–96 received a large amount of media coverage. In a dramatic way, the occurrences call to our attention the continuing divisions between the races. President Clinton himself spurred action to uncover any criminal acts related to these burnings. Some people have turned to Promise Keepers for answers because reconciliation has been a driving heartbeat for this organization. Promise Keepers was concerned that some of the damaged churches lacked adequate insurance, and it established a million-dollar fund to help rebuild these churches.

But even ten million dollars won't help if we don't reconcile on the personal level. As an organization Promise Keepers wants to do more than pour money into the situation. Promise Keepers is dedicated to uniting men in vital relationships to become godly influences to our world. This cause is paramount. Reconciling relationships means that we are moving beyond the physical walls of church barriers so that we can say to another man, "I will never violate you by burning your church or speaking against you. Whether I'm with you in body or not, you can count on me never to say a word against you." How can this promise be fulfilled in a world that says one thing, then lives another? But we can be certain because our relationships are Christ-centered and are driven with a spiritual basis.

In many places across America where the churches have burned, we see a genuine commitment and concern. This concern crosses racial and denominational lines to respond positively to those needs. While these churches will never be able to replace the heirlooms and historical documents that have been consumed by fire, they will be able to see the reality of 2 Corinthians 5:17 in their congregations. "The old has gone." These churches are now released from their old dependence on a building or a denomination or a relic from the past. Instead, "the new has come!" These fires have served to increase their faith in Christ Jesus, the bedrock of our salvation.

The new structures are being built with black hands, white hands, red hands, and brown hands—people from every race. The rebuilding of these church structures promotes a new sense of brotherhood and community that was unheard of in the past. While we cry—and rightly so—over the loss of these buildings that held such personal meaning for us, it is almost as though this act of violence toward the church is tearing down the walls that divide us.

MY COSTLY WAKE-UP CALL

ONE OF THE LESSONS I LEARNED about reconciliation was extremely costly. We named our church "All Nations" for the purpose of reaching across racial boundaries, but my focus personally was on becoming the bishop for Colorado in my denomination. At the denomination's annual convocation in Memphis one year, I had sought the position of bishop, but lost out on the appointment. Before I left the crucial meeting, I prayed, "Dear Lord, if I don't get to be appointed bishop of the state, please give me the city. I will be satisfied." Feeling forlorn and discouraged, I prepared to return to Denver. The night before the convocation concluded, I fell into a dream in which I could see my church building—on fire. An Egyptian sphinx rose out of the ashes of the church and stood like a monument from the rubble.

Suddenly, I woke up and began to search my Bible for a message from this dream. Through most of the night, I prayed and reflected on the dream's significance. The Lord gave me a title for my next sermon: "Up Out of the Ashes." I preached that message when I returned to my church the following Sunday. At the time, I thought the vision was a message about losing the position of bishop for Colorado and God's raising me up instead for a strong ministry. But God had a different explanation for my vision.

Two days after I preached that sermon, the church caught on fire. An old coal-burning furnace in our building had been converted into natural gas. We'd had some trouble with the pilot light even after the repairs were made. That night the burner got stuck on high, overheated the area, and caught on fire. We lost everything in a five-alarm fire in which three firemen were injured.

A television reporter asked me about the fire at the church. "Pastor, what are you going to do, now that your church has burned to the ground?"

I said, "You've missed it! The church of Jesus Christ cannot be burned. The building may burn, but the church didn't burn." Indeed, we had lost the physical expression of our church, but not the key part of it—the people. As we dug through the ashes of the building, the congregation came together in a fresh and wonderful way. In order to rebuild from the ashes, we needed each other.

ANOTHER KIND OF BARRIER

WHILE MUCH OF THIS CHAPTER has considered the barrier of racism, there is another wall that must also be removed on our path to purity: denominationalism.

Max Lucado, a prominent author, addressed the 44,000 pastors who attended the 1996 Promise Keepers Fan Into Flame Conference in Atlanta, Georgia. Lucado asked the audience to tell him a bit about themselves through shouting in unison the name of their particular church or denominational affiliation. The cacophonous words from the crowd were complete nonsense.

Then Lucado asked the audience, "On the count of three, state the name of the Messiah into whose arms you have entrusted your soul and to whom you have offered your sins and accepted His salvation." Together the men said the name "Jesus." The name stood in stark contrast to the confusion surrounding denominations and affiliations.

Lucado explained that God has enlisted us to serve on a battleship in a war and has given each of us a different task. The captain of our boat is Jesus, and our primary concern is not the strength of the ship but the harmony among the crew. There can be many opinions within the crew. One group is somber and serious. They are intent in their study of the words of the captain and occupy the section of the boat known as the stern. Another group is devoted to prayer and adopts a particular posture for prayer—kneeling—which is why these people are located in the bow of the boat. A different group is located near the engine of the ship, where they study the nuts and bolts of the situation on the premise that what you know is more important than what you feel.

Some people on the ship say that once you are on the boat, you can never get off. Others say, "You would be foolish to go overboard, but the choice is yours." Some of the crew believe you were recruited for service on the boat, while others believe you were destined for service before the boat was ever built.

There are those who speak to the captain in a personal prayer language, while others believe such a language no longer exists. ("Oh, how we cluster!" as Max Lucado put it.)

Some people think the officers should wear robes, and others think no one should wear them. Still another group believes that everyone is an officer and we should all wear robes.

The consequence of having all these groups on a battleship is that some people have chosen not to enter the boat. They say that while life is choppy on the open sea, they would rather face the waves than get caught between two fighting sailors.

Unfortunately, many of us have ignored the words that our captain, Jesus, uttered when He prayed for His disciples. During the final hours before His crucifixion, Jesus didn't pray for His disciples' health or happiness. Instead, He prayed for unity: "that all of them may be one, Father, just as you are in me and I am in you. May they also be in us so that the world may believe that you have sent me" (John 17:21).

Instead of unity, the church has been splintered into various denominations. Fortunately, in some parts of the church there is a fresh wind blowing. People like Chuck Colson have mobilized a movement to bring greater unity between evangelicals and Catholics. Through this movement we begin to celebrate what we hold in common rather than bicker about the aspects of our faith that divide us. Many of Colson's insights have been collected in a book called *Evangelicals and Catholics Together*, which he co-edited with Richard John Neuhaus (Word Books, 95). Sadly, Colson has come under fire for his efforts to bring unity to the church.

As Christians, we can agree on several basic tenets of the faith such as the veracity of the Word of God, the Bible, in its inerrant and original form. Other tenets that we hold in common are the deity of the Father God and the Son Jesus Christ, who was born of a virgin. We agree on the miracles that Jesus preformed and the fact of His sinless life. Finally, we celebrate the work of the Holy Spirit in our lives to help us live day to day and follow the example of Jesus Christ. These simple aspects of the faith we can hold in common—whether Protestant or Catholic.

As we make our way in a fragmented world—even within the church—we must follow a different path to purity. We can work for reconciliation across denominational and racial lines through a six-step process.

SIX STEPS TOWARD RECONCILIATION

IT IS NOT EASY TO WORK toward reconciliation between the races or denominations or across any other barrier. The barriers are not lowered quickly or through a solitary action. It takes years of effort and conscious decisions to make it happen. I have compressed the process of reconciliation into six steps. But this process has many variations and twists. To progress from level to level requires much diligent effort and prayer.

1. Confrontation. The first step is a bold one. It is only as we confront the differences—whether cultural, doctrinal, or ethnic—that we can truly begin the journey of reconciliation. Some people might question this: Aren't we already too aware of our differences, and isn't the point to emphasize what we have in common? Yes, but not until we really understand how we are different can we identify how much we have in common and see that our similarities go a lot deeper than our differences.

2. Compassion in Relationships. As we connect to the heart of God, we gain compassion for other people. Psalm 45:1 says,

> My heart is stirred by a noble theme
> as I recite my verses for the king;
> my tongue is the pen of a skillful writer.

The psalmist wrote some verses for the king, or the Creator, with a noble theme. He took the time to get to know God the Father and His love for mankind. He built a relationship with the Father and the Holy Spirit. A relationship as deep as this isn't just coincidence; it is deliberate.

The psalmist pondered what to write on the paper, then he composed it into moving verses. He thought about it deeply, settled it in his mind, and then was prepared to move ahead at all costs. By this means he developed compassion toward his fellow man. In the same way, we need to develop compassion for others—across racial and denominational barriers.

As Jesus comes into our lives and becomes present in our hearts, we become compassionate and caring people.

3. Consideration. After our hearts are softened and have become compassionate about reconciliation, we need to go to those with whom we seek to be reconciled and listen to their response. Listening doesn't come easy. We need to feel the pain that others have suffered on their journey to reconciliation. The response may not be easy to take. That other person, surprised at our overture, could feel stunned, unprepared, and overwhelmed. He could even be angry. Initially he may respond, "Yes, you did injure me. You injured my people. You injured my race. You didn't have to do that, but you did it." Be prepared for a negative response initially. But listen, nonetheless. As we listen, barriers between us will begin to fall down.

4. The Critical Moment. At this point, the initiator and the respondent evaluate where their relationship went off track. The initiator admits his failures and asks for forgiveness. The hurt person will either forgive the person or set down conditions for change. When we reach the critical moment in our relationships, we have taken a major step toward reconciliation.

5. Cement the Relationship. Sometimes the relationship will be sealed with a handshake or a hug from the injured party. If the injury to the other person is of a complex or compounded nature, you may have to write down the details of your plan for change and improvement in your relationship. Whatever course of action you take, be sure to seal and cement your relationship.

6. Continuity. How will your relationship continue to grow and improve? What sort of ongoing contact will you have with this person? The final step is to answer these important questions and devise a strategy for a continued relationship.

THE PLAN IN ACTION

WHILE IT MAY SEEM REASONABLE to condense the task of reconciliation into a six-step process, you may wonder how this is accomplished and put into practice. During the 1990 Promise Keepers conference, Coach McCartney spoke to 4,200 men in the basketball arena at the University of Colorado in Boulder. After completing his talk, Coach sat down, but felt the Holy Spirit say, "Look out at the audience and tell me what you see."

He looked around the arena and said, "Father, I praise God. I thank you for men."

But the Spirit prodded, "Look again at the color of the men. If you don't reach and get your brothers of color, then at next year's meeting when you come, I will not be here in my Shekinah glory." God *confronted* Coach Mac with the need for something different. Through this experience Coach Mac became sensitive to the need for racial reconciliation and the needs of men of color.

Coach Mac could well claim the words of the apostle Paul: "I was not disobedient to the vision from heaven" (Acts 26:19). In his heart, he heard the call and committed his lifework to the task of racial reconciliation. His heart grew with *compassion*.

Then Coach Mac began to talk about his vision for reconciliation first to those in the leadership of Promise Keepers and then beyond that. Promise Keepers made a commitment to reach over racial or denominational barriers to join hands with others. One day Coach Mac and other leaders from Promise Keepers came to my church. Naturally, they hoped that I would be open to the idea of joining their group. At the same time, they didn't know whether I would be willing to join them.

As I related earlier in this book, these men took the next step and elicited my response. It wasn't what they expected. I said, "What do you mean coming down here in my part of the city? You've come into the injured community, and you've injured us by dishonoring a young football player. You injured the black community who had gotten excited about a good player and a good team, but now you've suspended him. We don't like it, and we're trying to see what we can do to let you know we don't like it." I gave my response, and Coach *considered* it.

The *critical moment* arrived when Coach Mac began to explain his perspective on the suspension. As he recited the specific rules, Coach denied that the decision was based on prejudice or discrimination. But when he saw my look of disbelief, he pondered his words and realized that behind the suspension lay some prejudicial actions against African American players. Minority players were being arrested in Boulder County at an alarming rate. Moreover, they were being treated differently from whites during their arrest. Coach Mac's critical moment came when he understood the injury—whether real or perceived.

As I looked at the situation with the honesty required at such a moment, I understood that I, along with the rest of my African American community, had acted emotionally out of a judgmental attitude. We based our judgment on the fact that the coach was a white man and the young football player was a black man. For our part, we didn't allow for rules and regulations governing the suspension. This critical moment brought a review in the heart of the coach ("the oppressor"), and also in my heart ("the oppressed").

After this critical moment, Coach and I vowed to act. We repented to each other. The coach asked forgiveness for not looking into the rules to see how they could be prejudicial toward African American players. I repented for not allowing that there was a set of rules and operating procedures under which the coach was working. This critical moment involved introspection.

Thus we began to *cement* a relationship with repentance. We affirmed each other's integrity. This event marked the beginning of our long-term relationship.

So our relationship has had the *continuity* that is crucial to the reconciliation process. On the one hand, Coach Mac and the leadership of Promise Keepers offered me a seat on the board of directors. On the other hand, I have confirmed the relationship by my belief in their program and my desire to serve them as brothers in Christ. At first, I had to answer to my African American community and get their approval and consent to join this fast-growing men's movement. Eventually that community understood the motives and goals of this group and gave me permission to join the board. Reconciliation is not an instant process, but a gradual one that requires continuity.

Today Coach Mac and I meet together often. We pray for each other and stand in support of each other, even when we're apart. I know that I can count on Bill to cover my back, and he can count on me to cover his. When I'm with a group of African Americans and he's not with us, Coach knows that I'm not going to shoot him down. When he is with a group of whites, I know Coach is not going to shoot me down. We also communicate with and affirm each other through notes and cards. As in any relationship, we don't always agree on every point. But we've come to know the depth of the other person's heart and his integrity.

IT'S YOUR CHOICE

AS YOU HAVE SEEN, the path of reconciliation and moving beyond the barriers of race and denomination has not been easy for me. Some people ask me, "Phil, aren't you bitter from the rejection of your first job? And what about when your father's butt was kicked in that grocery store?"

From my spiritual experience, I know that each of those defining moments in life required that I make a critical choice. I could turn bitter and let revenge and violence fill my life. I tried that for a while through boxing and fighting, but that brought no sense of fulfillment. We all pass through experiences that bring defining moments. The wise course is to try to be prepared for such experiences and even plan our response. I have decided and have made a commitment that when I confront a difficult situation, I will try to reach beyond any racial or denominational barriers and seek to demonstrate the power of biblical unity as I walk along this path to purity. Through my experiences, I have seen God honor this choice in my life.

STRAIGHT TO THE PATH

1. Evaluate your friendships. Do they cross racial and denominational lines? What steps can you take to break down barriers and promote understanding?
2. Consider your feelings of prejudice. Are they directed toward races? Toward people who hold a different set of religious beliefs? How can you celebrate the ways you are similar instead of the ways you are different?
3. Review the six steps of the process of reconciliation.

    Confrontation: How have you been confronted with your need for reconciliation?

    Compassion: How are you growing in compassion for others? How are you nurturing compassion for the people around you?

    Consideration: Are you prepared to listen to others and thereby share their pain? Evaluate your listening skills and develop a plan for improvement.

    Critical Moment: Is there a relationship that needs the kind of evaluation that will bring you to a critical moment? Do you and the other person see where your relationship went off track? Take the initiative and confront the situation so as to help tear down the wall that divides.

Cement: Is there a relationship that needs some cement? If you feel that you are approaching the critical moment, what can you do to solidify and strengthen the relationship after that moment is passed?

Continuity: How have you modeled continuity in a relationship? What can you do more consistently to strengthen a particular relationship? Make it a point to express to the other person your appreciation or desire for continuity. An attitude of gratitude goes a long way in the process of reconciliation.

4. I have used the example of Coach Bill McCartney to show how he and I walked through this reconciliation process. Has this process worked for you? Have you gone through it from start to finish? If so, make some notes about your experience, then talk it over with a friend. The fact that you have started on the journey will be an encouragement to you *and* your friend.

Perhaps, in reading this chapter, you have become aware of a need for reconciliation. Create a plan of action for working through the six steps. Record your progress at each step. This record will be an encouragement to continue along the path of purity.

CHAPTER EIGHT

ONE MAN CAN MAKE A DIFFERENCE IN HIS WORLD

TOM TARRANTS FILLED HIS LIFE with hate for blacks and Jews. As a young man in Mississippi, Tarrants joined the Ku Klux Klan and found in it an outlet for venting his hatred. Eventually, the police caught Tom in some Klan-related activities, and he ended up on Death Row at Parchman Prison in Mississippi. His world shrank to a six-by-nine-foot cell. Out of sheer boredom, Tom began to read everything he could get his hands on—including a Bible.

Even with his hate-filled activities, Tom had considered himself a Christian, but he never enjoyed reading the Bible. He used a few verses out of context to support his neo-Nazi, racist beliefs, but for the most part, he had found the Bible boring and difficult to understand. Now, languishing in prison, Tom found that the words leaped off the page. In the book *He's My Brother,* Tom describes what happened: "The more I read, the more convinced I became that I was lost, separated from God by my sin. . . . As I read the sixteenth chapter of Matthew, one verse in particular burned its way into my soul, 'For what shall it profit a man, if he shall gain the whole world, and lose his soul?'" As if under a search-light, Tom could see the hatred in his life for the first time. He writes, "Seeing my own wickedness in the light of the love of God broke me completely, and I wept like a baby. . . . I was still locked in a tiny prison cell. But for the first time in my life, I was free" (John Perkins and Thomas A. Tarrants, *He's My Brother: Former Racial Foes Offer Strategy for Reconciliation* [Baker, 1994]).

God's love broke through the barrier of hatred in Tom's life, and today Tom is the pastor of an interracial church in Washington, D.C. Tom discovered the final path to purity. As he began to obey the Great Commandment, he found a commitment to influence his world for Jesus Christ.

In chapter 2 I discussed the importance of following Jesus Christ with all your heart. Jesus pinpointed the Great Commandment in Mark 12:30–31: "'Love the Lord your God with all your heart and with all your soul and with all your mind and with all your strength.' The second [commandment] is this: 'Love your neighbor as yourself.' There is no commandment greater than these."

We find it easy to love ourselves and to center the world around *our* wishes and *our* desires. To see the self-centered perspective of the world, we only have to think about the ads on television. "You deserve a break today . . ." and countless variations on that theme emphasize that the world should revolve around us as individuals. But as we follow God's direction and the last path to purity, we rise above our desires and wishes and turn our focus on our neighbors and friends.

In his book *How to Make People Really Feel Loved . . . And Other Life-giving Observations* (Vine Books, 1997), Charlie

W. Shedd tells about a big fellow who had never finished high school but was greatly loved in his church and construction business. People flocked around this man, and Charlie asked him for the secret of his love from and for others. The man replied, "You've got to break the habit of thinking of yourself first. But if you can turn your mind in this direction, you'll discover there really is something special in every person. And the more you practice looking for the good in others, the more you will see it quick."

Then the man concluded his discourse with this gem: "The secret is to find the good things and to give them back. I mean out loud, sincere, and very strong. If you will do this and keep on till it comes easy, then another beautiful thing happens. One day you'll begin to really love people like the Bible says you should."

To focus on the good in others takes a wholehearted commitment.

SIX WAYS TO LOVE YOUR NEIGHBOR

In a society that tends to breed isolation, it is sad that many of us never really get acquainted with our neighbors. Like separate little islands, we live with our families, go to work, go to church, go on vacation—but never take the time to go next door. If we want to influence the world, we first need to be influencing the people in our immediate range of contact. If we have never tried it, here are some ways to start.

1. Take specific actions to become friends with your neighbors. Holidays such as Easter and Christmas and the Fourth of July can provide opportunities. Invite neighbors to your home for a cookout or a dessert social; you don't have to make it a religious event. The important thing as

you interact with your neighbors is that they see that you care about them as individuals. Can you help in some practical way such as lending a tool or helping them with a skill?

2. If you don't want to entertain, you can make a dessert or cookies and give them to a neighbor.

3. Make a point to greet your neighbors when they enter or leave their home. Speak to them if you pass within earshot, and learn their names. An old Chinese proverb says, "He who wants friends must be friendly."

4. As you develop friendships with your neighbors, you will have natural opportunities to talk about your faith. Pray that God will open up such occasions, and then, as it feels natural, weave spiritual matters into your conversation. Joseph C. Aldrich has written some excellent guidelines on this topic in his book *Lifestyle Evangelism* (Multnomah Press, 1983).

5. For a broader impact on your community, consider organizing a Serve the City program. Promise Keepers started this program with the goal to foster relationships across denominational and racial lines. In fall 1996, more than three hundred volunteers in the Denver area worked on twenty-one different projects. Men took the time on Saturdays usually reserved for golf or family activities to work in small groups on projects such as hanging drywall in churches or painting rooms or installing carpets. Other Serve the City programs have been held in Dallas, Detroit, Washington, and Oakland. The beauty of the program is the opportunity it gives to men for building relationships with people with whom they might not normally come in contact. Serve the City is a practical program that can serve as a model for other communities.

6. Work on a Habitat for Humanity building project. Many communities in the United States have a local Habi-

tat for Humanity office. Former president Jimmy Carter has been active in this organization which organizes churches or other groups for the purpose of building or refurbishing homes for the disadvantaged. The projects are short term and aren't limited to people with professional building skills. Much of the work entails no more than using a paint-brush or hauling bricks or other forms of manual labor. If you have a particular trade such as plumbing or drywalling, you can, of course, make an essential contribution to the project. Constructing these homes offers a ready-made opportunity to serve your community and work shoulder to shoulder with people from other churches, races, or economic conditions.

As you love your neighborhood with the love of Jesus Christ, you will begin to influence your community—but don't stop there. Let us continue on this final path to purity and learn how we can change the focus in our jobs from success to significance.

TASTE SUCCESS, THEN FIND SIGNIFICANCE

FRED BRAHNSON KNEW HOW TO BE SERVED. As a child in North Carolina, his parents had black servants in the home. After graduating from the University of North Carolina, Fred continued on into medical school. During his training, he was shocked one day to meet a black doctor. It came as a surprise to this southern man that black people could have what it takes to become physicians.

To establish his medical practice, Fred and his wife Julie moved to Boseman, Montana, and quickly developed a flourishing medical practice. His wife seemed extremely happy in their new, large home. As his career prospered, Fred's spiritual life was also growing, and he was beginning to look for ways to fulfill the Great Commandment and the Great Commission.

Then one day as he was praying, Fred felt a strong urging from the Lord to move to Africa and continue his medical work there.

"You can't be serious, God!" Fred responded. "We just finished our home, and I don't think Julie is remotely interested in going to Africa." Instead of talking it over with Julie, Dr. Brahnson kept praying about what to do next with his life. He had success, but he was wondering how to find significance. It seemed that Africa offered a partial answer to his questions.

Several days later, Julie woke with a start in the middle of the night. She stirred her sleeping husband and said, "Honey, you have to listen to me! God told me to sell the house and go into missionary work."

Fred could only smile at God's humor and guidance.

Before long, the Brahnsons sold their home and medical practice and indeed moved to Nigeria. After a couple of years, the Brahnsons and their Nigerian-born daughter, returned to Boseman. On one of my periodic trips to Montana in the course of my duties as bishop, I met the Brahnsons. We have become dear friends.

Recently, life for the Brahnsons took another twist in their seeking to follow God's will. They moved to Mendenhall, Mississippi, where they now work with lower-income African Americans and provide medical treatment for people who can't afford it. This is quite a shift from Fred's childhood, when all the blacks he knew were servants. Dr. Brahnson has seen his life journey move from success to significance. Each day is an adventure as he seeks to follow the Great Commission and "go into all the world."

While God may not call *you* to Africa or to Mendenhall, Mississippi, as you are learning to love your neighbor, He may take you in a different direction in terms of your career, or He may ask you to devote several weeks in a summer to Christian service. Are you willing to use your skills for God's kingdom? Your answer is important to this final path to purity in which you are committed to influencing your world for Jesus Christ.

EXPAND YOUR WORLD THROUGH PRAYER

YEARS AGO, DR. BRUCE WILKERSON, a friend and the founder of Walk Thru the Bible Ministries, began to pray about enlarging the borders of his life. While attending Dallas Theological Seminary, Bruce came upon a couple of short verses in 1 Chronicles. These verses were mingled in with a long, uninteresting genealogy. There was a man called Jabez. First Chronicles 4:9–10 says, "Jabez was more honorable than his brothers. His mother had named him Jabez, saying, 'I gave birth to him in pain.' Jabez cried out to the God of Israel, 'Oh, that you would bless me and enlarge my territory! Let your hand be with me, and keep me from harm so that I will be free from pain.' And God granted his request."

Bruce wondered what God would accomplish in his life if he adopted this prayer of Jabez. Bruce adopted the verse as his "life verse" and began to teach creative seminars so that people could more easily learn the major events of the Bible. His work eventually grew to become the international ministry called Walk Thru the Bible.

God continues to answer Bruce's prayers and enlarge his borders. What would happen in your life if you began to pray toward such an end? Expect God to honor your faith.

Prayer was the means God used to expand my own ideas about the world. A number of years ago, I encouraged my congregation to start praying about reaching out to the world. Together we began to pray through the words of Isaiah 43:5–6:

> "Do not be afraid, for I am with you;
>> I will bring your children from the east
>> and gather you from the west.
> I will say to the north, 'Give them up!'
>> and to the south, 'Do not hold them back.'
> Bring my sons from afar
>> and my daughters from the ends of the earth."

The church prayed first for our own city of Aurora. Then the focus of our prayer widened to include Denver, then Jefferson County, then across the Rocky Mountains to Utah, Nevada, and California. As we continued to pray, we enlarged our prayers to include Asia and the Pacific Ocean. In the same fashion, we turned to the east, the north, and the south. Our interest in world affairs increased, and our borders were enlarged.

In 1987, I received a call from the Immigration and Naturalization Service (INS): "Would your church be interested in sponsoring some Ethiopian Pentecostals emigrating to the United States?" The congregation embraced the idea of sponsorship with enthusiasm. Our church helped about fourteen people learn English and find homes and jobs in the Denver area. A couple of these people, Endeshaw and Genetta, became pastors to other Ethiopians who emigrated to Denver later on.

Our church family continued to pray in the spirit of Isaiah 43 and ask God to fulfill those verses through us. A couple of years later, the INS asked us to sponsor some Russian Pentecostal refugees. Because our experience with the Ethiopians had gone so well, we agreed once again. To our surprise, we were sent twenty-seven Russian refugees to be housed in the basement of our church!

Immediately there was a problem. The refugees spoke no English and, of course, we spoke no Russian. We are black; they were of a lighter hue. Even our styles of worship were different. All Nations Church is quite vocal and exhibits much jubilance and praise. The Russian Pentecostals believed that true spirituality is expressed in quiet piety. At the beginning, our relationship was awkward and tentative.

But the end result was a tremendous blessing. Through acts of kindness in providing food, clothing, shelter, and jobs, along with assisting the people with their immigration paperwork, we built a great friendship. Eventually they formed their own Russian Pentecostal church in the Denver area.

Our actions toward the Russians and the Ethiopians didn't come naturally. Rather, we responded because of our relationship with God and our desire to see the world touched for Jesus Christ. During His final moments on earth, Jesus gave His disciples what is commonly known as the Great Commission: "All authority in heaven and on earth has been given to me. Therefore go and make disciples of all nations, baptizing them in the name of the Father and of the Son and of the Holy Spirit, and teaching them to obey everything I have commanded you. And surely I am with you always, to the very end of the age" (Matthew 28:18–20). Many spiritual people are trying to follow this command and evangelize the world. If we are to be men who follow the final path to purity, we have to move beyond the Great Commandment and follow the Great Commission in order to influence our world.

FIVE WAYS TO INFLUENCE YOUR WORLD

FROM SHEER NUMBERS, IT SEEMS IMPOSSIBLE to have any influence on the world. There are billions of people on this planet, and our life passes in the blink of an eye. Yet, on our final path to purity, I believe we can have a profound impact on the world around us. Here are five means to accomplish that goal:

1. Pray for the world consistently. I am not talking about the simple prayer that many tack onto "grace" at mealtime: "Lord, bless all of the missionaries. Amen." We need to be praying for the *world*—specifically, for various needs. An excellent tool for learning about the needs of the world is *Operation World* by Patrick Johnstone (Zondervan, 1993). This book gives a day-by-day guide for prayer along with a comprehensive guide with statistics and up-to-date information about various nations and people groups. Another method is simply to use a map of the world and begin praying specifically for each nation.

2. Make friends with an international student in your community. Many world leaders have received their college education in the United States. For example, Prime Minister Benjamin Netanyahu from Israel studied at Massachusetts Institute of Technology (MIT). Unfortunately, 80 percent of these students never entered an American home.

Strategic friendships with international students can make a tremendous difference in the shape of our world in the years to come. Even if a student doesn't live in your home, there are many ways to absorb him or her into the fabric of everyday life. One resource for information is International Students, Inc. (1–800-ISI-TEAM or E-mail ISITEAM@aol.com). Another aid is the book *The World at Your Door: Reaching International Students in Your Home, Church and School* by Dr. Tom Phillips, Bob Norsworthy and W. Terry Whalin (Bethany House Publishers, 1997).

International friendships will broaden your perspective on the world and help you fulfill the Great Commission.

3. Entertain missionaries in your home. Particularly in the summertime, many missionaries return from their place of service and travel around the United States, reporting to churches. Volunteer at the next opportunity to have one of these missionaries and his or her family in your home. Make a conscious effort to ask good questions and listen to these missionaries.

This experience will broaden your view of the world and also give you a chance to be an encourager for these servants of God. Unfortunately, many missionaries feel that they are not listened to or encouraged when they return to the home country; they too often find church members absorbed with their own concerns.

4. Be a sender—give and correspond faithfully with missionaries. These servants of Christ need people who will care about them consistently. They need people who will assist financially and also correspond with them and pray faithfully for them. You can influence your world by having a consistent involvement with missionaries. It will also bless your own life as you pray and see answers to prayer through them.

5. Learn about other parts of the world firsthand. Consider undertaking a short-term missions trip. A number of missions agencies and churches offer this opportunity. Your skills can be well put to use in a temporary situation. Such a venture will give you a fresh perspective on the world and

a greater appreciation for your homeland. A helpful resource is *The Complete Student Missions Handbook* by Ridge Burns with Noel Becchetti (Zondervan, 1990). This resource will give you a step-by-step guide to leading a group from the classroom to the mission field.

REAFFIRM GOD AS THE CEO OF YOUR LIFE

WE WILL NEVER REACH OUT AND touch the world for Jesus Christ until we fall in love with God and make Him the Chief Executive Officer of our lives. God will never force Himself on us, but when we willingly turn to Him, He is able to use us. In the same way, we can submit our lives to the Chief Operating Officer—the Holy Spirit. The COO has the continuing responsibility to the President of the Corporation—Jesus Christ.

You may be a businessman or a teacher or a laborer or a doctor or something else. Your training, your schooling, your motivations, and your goals all pointed you toward a career. You knew where you wanted to go. Spiritually, we also need to know where we want to go. We can go against God's direction for our lives, but that is unnatural. The natural course is to turn every day toward God and ask for His direction. Then we can live in the strength of the Spirit and not in our own strength.

We don't know the future. Tomorrow may bring tremendous blessing or tremendous calamity. We can't see the end of the path of purity, so instead, we all have to hold to the seven key principles for living. As we follow these spiritual solutions to everyday problems, we can touch the world for Jesus Christ and our impact will exceed any of our dreams.

STRAIGHT TO THE PATH ───────────────

1. Review "Six Ways to Love Your Neighbor." Does one particular way stand out in your mind—something that you feel motivated to accomplish? Set a goal to apply this strategy and influence your neighbors for Christ.

2. Review "Five Ways to Influence Your World." Select one method and begin working on it. It is only as we are on the move for God that He can use us to influence our world.

3. How are you enlarging your borders through prayer? Follow the example of Jabez from 1 Chronicles and see how God will enlarge the borders of your world and the borders of your influence in the name of Christ.

CHAPTER NINE

The Most Important Path

IN THESE PAGES YOU HAVE TRAVELED with me along the path to purity. You have seen my struggles to remain on the path to purity as I encountered different bumps along the road. Often I think my path is completely laid out, and then I make an unexpected turn. For example, I had intended to study at Lincoln University under a full scholarship—but instead, I integrated Phillips University in my hometown of Enid. On another occasion, I thought my career as a social worker was completely planned and sealed, but then my job was canceled because I am an African American. These experiences and others like them define who I am today and my current role as the pastor of All Nations Church, the Bishop of Montana, and the chairman of the board for Promise Keepers.

I have learned a critical lesson along the path to purity: It is impossible to understand who you are without knowing where you came from. We all need to examine our path to purity and survey the road we have traveled to arrive at this point in time. The early pages of Genesis give some insight about our origins. We were a lifeless lump of clay until God breathed in us and made us a living soul. The Creator of the Universe made man in His own image. We were created with a spiritual connection, and it is crucial that we understand this spiritual side of life.

Ours is in many ways a plastic world. Plastic often serves as an imitation or substitute for something "real," such as hard metal. In the same way, people may think they have a true relationship, only to discover that the relationship is fake or plastic. American society has for many taken on a dog-eat-dog, get-ahead-at-all-costs mentality. Yet when men have clawed and gnawed their way to the pinnacle of life, they find themselves self-centered and lonely. Instead of the lush forest and landscapes they thought they would see, there is nothing below but a vast wasteland. And they still don't have an answer to the most critical question: Which path do I choose for my life?

In Deuteronomy 8:2–3, Moses reminded the Jewish people of the need to remember the importance of a relationship with God:

> Remember how the LORD your God led you all the way in the desert these forty years, to humble you and to test you in order to know what was in your heart, whether or not you would keep his commands. He humbled you, causing you to hunger and then feeding you with manna, which neither you nor your fathers had known, to teach you that man does not live on bread alone but on every word that comes from the mouth of the LORD.

As we look through history, different leaders have risen to meet the challenge of their day—men such as Franklin D. Roosevelt, Winston Churchill, John F. Kennedy, Martin

Luther King Jr., and Nelson Mandela. Each of these men addressed a pressing need of their times with vision, courage, and commitment. Whatever their faith, that mission was essentially spiritual at its heart. Through Promise Keepers, I have seen men across the United States and around the world struggle with similar issues of spirituality. Are men leaders or leeches? Wimps or winners? What are the standards or absolutes to follow in life? Where do you find these standards for life spelled out?

Even as Promise Keepers was bringing thousands of men together into large stadiums across the United States, Louis Farrakhan and the Nation of Islam were able to gather thousands of African Americans in Washington, D.C., in 1995 for the "Million Man March." From my perspective, Farrakhan's gathering showed the hunger among men to have a leader. Farrakhan is attractive because he challenges leadership in a flamboyant and arrogant style. The response he received suggests to me that black men throughout America feel forsaken by their political party, the social system, the justice system, the educational system, and the economic system. Farrakhan touches a spiritually sensitive chord and a desire for political power. Yet there is no way that I will attend any gathering on behalf of the Nation of Islam. It is not the path that leads to the correct answer to our daily problems.

Even before the Million Man March, Promise Keepers was considering holding a large rally of its own in Washington, and that plan was finally fulfilled on October 4, 1997. We gathered, not for a political purpose, but to call men to spiritual renewal. Promise Keepers is not political in nature and is not aligned with a particular political party or persuasion; the movement is focused on seven different promises relating to spiritual living. Nor was the gathering solely for African Americans. Instead, men from across racial and denominational lines came together for this unusual event.

What better place to demonstrate the unity and integrity of men than in the nation's capital? The meeting was called "Stand in the Gap: A Sacred Assembly of Men." The theme was based on Ezekiel 22:30: "I looked for a man among them who would build up the wall and stand before me in the gap on behalf of the land so I would not have to destroy it, but I found none."

From biblical times to the early centuries of the church and into the present day, there has been a consistent pattern among God's people—a progression from departure from God, judgment by God, a return to God, and revival by God. In the Old Testament, a "sacred assembly" was often the occasion to start a revival (see Nehemiah 8; also, Leviticus 23; Numbers 28). The last major revival to come to America was the Prayer Revival of 1857–58, and it originated with a series of "union prayer meetings." As the country awakened to the need for revival, it is estimated that nearly one million people accepted Jesus Christ.

The main focus of Stand in the Gap was prayer, worship, confession, repentance, and reconciliation. As individuals and as a nation, we have stepped off the path to purity and pursued our own interests and desires, instead of God's. Uniting as men, we are turning back toward the spiritual connection and centrality of our relationship with the God of the Universe through Jesus Christ. Stand in the Gap was also a time of rededication. We all need to rededicate our lives first of all to God, then to our families, and finally to the nation. This gathering expressed a commitment to proclaim the lordship of Jesus Christ over every aspect of life. It transcended any political purpose, and millions of men were taking a stand before the nation to declare their commitment to integrity.

Perhaps this Stand in the Gap experience is a foretaste of heaven. The apostle John wrote about heaven in the final book of the Bible: "After this I looked and there before me was a great multitude that no one could count, from every nation, tribe, people and language, standing before the throne and in front of the Lamb" (Revelation 7:9). People from every race were standing in front of Jesus Christ. We gained a taste of that experience in the nation's capital with men from every race and color.

PATHS TO THE RIVER OF LIFE

AS YOU HAVE SEEN IN THIS BOOK, the seven different paths to purity are not separate strands. Rather, each path builds on the next path. The *first* path involves having a life committed to Jesus Christ and the Bible. As I built my life on this path, it gave reason and increased motivation to follow the *second* path to purity—accountability with a small group of men. With this increased relationship with men, I am able to follow the *third* path—a life of integrity with spiritual, ethical, sexual, and moral purity. When I live with this type of integrity, then I'm able to increase my commitment to my greatest investment—my wife and my children. So the family is the *fourth* path to purity. Because I am committed to building a strong family, I need a place to grow and increase my spiritual relationship. Therefore the *fifth* path to purity is my support of the local church and the pastor of that house of God. Because of my love for Jesus, I can commit my time and resources to the work of the church. The *sixth* path has been a critical part of my life—reconciliation among races and denominations. It is only as I have traveled the other five paths that I am really ready and able to reach across the barriers of race or denominations and touch people with the power of our unity in Christ. A natural outgrowth of this is the *seventh* path to purity—a commitment to the Great Commandment and the Great Commission.

I picture these seven paths as a river. A small stream (my spiritual commitment) rushes down a mountainside, and another stream merges into it (the strength of a small group). The first stream gains momentum and power because of the second stream. As the water continues to flow down the mountain, a third stream (a commitment to purity) is added. Then comes a fourth (marriage and family relationships) as the stream turns into a river of life. The fifth stream (a connection with a local church) adds another power boost to the rushing water. The river grows larger still (through a commitment to break down the barriers of race and denomination), and finally it merges with a seventh stream (a vision to reach the world for Jesus Christ). These seven merged streams have become a single force that is not easily divided or impeded.

The seven paths to purity become a guide for living that can transform us from the inside out and make us a force in this world that perhaps we never thought we could be.

STEPPING OFF THE PATH

I HAVE EXPLAINED THAT THE CHURCH has been a central part of my life from my earliest memories. As the son of a pastor, I found it quite natural to pursue spiritual solutions to problems and obstacles. Some of my greatest moments with the Lord came during my youth. I spent a great deal of time in prayer and church services and reading the Bible. Then one day my steps took a different direction—a turn not uncommon among people who have grown up in a religious family. I decided to put religion aside and try to live without a spiritual basis. I stepped off the path of purity.

I have recounted my experiences in public speaking when I was a teenager. I found I loved to hold people spellbound with my oratory skills, whether in a church or in speaking to predominantly white groups and civic clubs in my hometown of Enid, Oklahoma.

Besides speaking, I learned to use my fists effectively. With a sense of satisfaction, I would lace on a pair of boxing gloves and step into the ring. It was a legal way to express my hatred and displeasure over racism—being able to pound the face of an opponent, be he white or black. When the crowd cheered at my victories, I loved it and felt affirmed as a young man. Upon earning a Golden Gloves title as a middleweight, I became something of a local celebrity in the press. In those days of segregation, my boxing was bringing me adulation as an African American.

As my success in speaking and boxing grew, however, I was spending less and less time at prayer meetings, reading the Bible, or attending church services.

And I still felt empty and unfulfilled. The plaudits of other people didn't bring the satisfaction I was seeking. I had strayed from the path of purity.

Many people have made such a journey, seeking to find fulfillment in a career or wealth or education or sex or alcohol or elsewhere. But instead of a deepening sense of pleasure, they find only false hope and emptiness.

One afternoon, I took a walk and reflected on my boxing success. The night before, I had heard an evangelist, and his message seemed to be directed right at me. "There is only one way to the spiritual life," the evangelist said. He quoted the words of Jesus in John 14:6–7: "I am the way, the truth and the life. No one comes to the Father except through me. If you really knew me, you would know my Father as well. From now on, you do know him and have seen him."

I sensed the reality of those words. Apart from Christ, there is no life or truth. That evening, when the evangelist gave the altar call, I walked to the front of the church and took a public and irrevocable step back to the path of purity.

WELCOME ARMS OF MERCY

AMID THE HARRIED BUSINESS OF LIVING, you may feel as if you have stepped off the path. You may be thinking, "Oh, Bishop Porter, you don't know the kind of terrible life I've led. The way I have pursued success or have fallen morally. . . ." The Bible makes it clear that everyone has sinned and strayed from the path. The prophet Isaiah compared our lives to sheep: "We all, like sheep, have gone astray, each of us has turned to his own way; and the LORD has laid on him the iniquity of us all" (Isaiah 53:6).

Whatever path has led you away from Jesus Christ, you can correct it and return to the path of purity and spiritual pursuits. The Creator God and Jesus Christ are waiting with open arms to welcome you, *but* Jesus will never force His way into your life. He declared in Revelation 3:20, "Here I am! I stand at the door and knock. If anyone hears my voice and opens the door [that is, returns to the path], I will come in and eat with him, and he with me."

Forgiveness, grace, and mercy are continually available on the path to purity. No matter how far you have strayed and no matter what you have done, you can discover the blessings of a life given to the pursuit of purity.

As you have seen, my difficulties did not disappear when I got back on the path to purity. I have encountered my share of obstacles on the way. The good news is that we don't have to face these obstacles alone. We can walk the path with the strongest partner in the universe: Jesus Christ. God called King David a "man after my own heart" (Acts 13:22; see 1 Samuel 13:14). As a young man, David developed an intense love for God and sought to follow God's commands and teaching. David wrote about purity:

> How can a young man keep his way pure?
>   By living according to your word.
> I seek you with all my heart;
>   do not let me stray from your commands.
> I have hidden your word in my heart
>   that I might not sin against you. (Psalm 119:9–11)

Life deals to each of us disappointments and difficulties. The path to purity is marked by a life committed to Jesus Christ and a daily obedience to the truth of the Bible.

Two thousand years ago, the course of human history changed forever. The sky was aglow with angels singing, "Glory to God in the highest, and on earth peace to men on whom his favor rests" (Luke 2:14). In a small stable in Bethlehem, Jesus Christ was born to the virgin Mary. As He walked the face of the earth, Jesus performed miracles and fulfilled many prophecies predicted about His life. Beyond His acts of ministry and teaching during three years, Jesus performed the greatest miracle of all. He took my sins and mistakes along with the sins of the world to a horrible death on the cross. When Jesus died, saying, "Father, into your hands I commit my spirit," the earth shook and the huge veil in the temple that set off the Holy of Holies split into two pieces (see Luke 23:44–46). Three days later, Jesus rose from the dead.

We have no good reason to pursue emptiness, shallow success, or a hollow career. Jesus Christ can guide us on a path that makes life worth living. And He will walk along that pathway with us. I have committed my life to staying on the path to purity. That path of purity is the *only* viable course in a fallen world that is out of control.

We want to hear from you. Please send your comments about this book to us in care of the address below. Thank you.

ZondervanPublishingHouse
Grand Rapids, Michigan 49530
http://www.zondervan.com